# Sailboat Church

# Sailboat Church

## Helping Your Church Rethink Its Mission and Practice

*Joan S. Gray*

WESTMINSTER
JOHN KNOX PRESS
LOUISVILLE • KENTUCKY

*First edition*
Published by Westminster John Knox Press
Louisville, Kentucky

14 15 16 17 18 19 20 21 22 23—10 9 8 7 6 5 4 3 2 1

*Book design by Sharon Adams*
*Cover design by Dilu Nicholas*

**Library of Congress Cataloging-in-Publication Data**

Gray, Joan S. (Joan Standridge), 1952–
Sailboat church : helping your church rethink its mission and practice / Joan S. Gray. —
First edition.
    pages cm
Includes bibliographical references.
ISBN 978-0-664-25958-7 (alk. paper)
1. Mission of the church—United States. 2. Church renewal—United States. 3. Church
growth—United States. 4. Church work—United States. 5. Boats and boating—Miscellanea.
I. Title.
BV601.8.G73 2014
253—dc23

                                                                    2013041194

♾ The paper used in this publication meets the minimum requirements of the
American National Standard for Information Sciences—Permanence of
Paper for Printed Library Materials, ANSI Z39.48-1992.

Most Westminster John Knox Press books are available at special quantity discounts when
purchased in bulk by corporations, organizations, and special-interest groups. For more
information, please e-mail SpecialSales@wjkbooks.com.

Dedicated to
All the churches who have sailed with me
during my years of ministry, especially to the congregation
and session of Clairmont Presbyterian Church
who helped pray this book to completion.

# Contents

# Acknowledgments

$T$his book never would have been started without the inspiration and partnership of B. J. Woodworth. He would have been coauthor of *Sailboat Church* if his "sailing duties" at the Open Door Church in Pittsburgh, Pennsylvania, had not sent him in other directions. I very much appreciate the encouragement of Cecil Murphey, surely the most generous mentor of writers ever. I am also indebted to those folks who took time to read and make extensive comments on the manuscript in the early stages. You will see I took your comments seriously. Deepest thanks to my husband, Bill, always my first reader and editor, and to all the people who helped pray this book into existence, especially the Girlfriends.

# Introduction

*I*t is a warm summer day at the lake. The water looks cool and inviting. You push your boat off the shore, pick up the oars, and begin to row over to the other side. After a while what seemed like a warm day begins to feel hot. Pulling at the oars, your arms begin to tire, and the other shore looks farther away than when you started. You stop for a moment to rest, and as you wipe the sweat off your face, you see a *Sailboat* on the lake, not too far off. It is skimming across the water, almost dancing with the wind. The Sailboat is coming in your direction. You admire its graceful movement. As you pick up the oars again, you wonder what it would be like to sail.

⸙ ⸙ ⸙ ⸙ ⸙ ⸙

Many North American Christians have spent their whole lives in churches that operate mainly by rowing. Rowboat churches do what they can with the resources—money, wisdom, energy, people, facilities—they have. In a time when church was a respected fixture of our culture and a major center of community life, this approach often took the church a long way. Today, however, many rowboat churches are finding that rowing is not getting them where they want to go. This situation has painful symptoms.

In many congregations the number of members is stagnant or decreasing at a steady rate. Older members die or become disabled, and no one takes their place. Other congregations struggle to fund programs, mission, and building upkeep with lower budgets than they used to have. Painful cuts have to be made. Significant numbers of churches are made up of people who once lived nearby but who have now moved away and travel some distance to worship. The surrounding community does not really seem interested in the best they have to offer. They mourn the loss of children and youth in the church, and no one can remember the last time there was an adult baptism. As the pool of members decreases, it is tough to find people to serve on church boards.

Distress is also seen in the lives and ministry of clergy serving these churches. Declining churches often take out their unhappiness on their leaders. The culture of respect that once surrounded the office of clergy has evaporated. Members of declining congregations often have the unrealistic expectation that the right pastor can solve all their problems. This can set up both clergy and congregations for disappointment. Older clergy sometimes feel that the rules of ministry have changed and what is expected of them today is not what they were trained to do. Younger clergy say that their dreams and visions often don't fit into an institutional pattern that looks back to the glory days of the 1950s.

Even Christians whose congregations still have plenty of resources and members sense that things have changed. It used to be the norm that when people started a family or moved to a new community, they looked for a church. Now they are more likely to look for the nearest mall or coffee shop on Sunday mornings. People do not "fall in" the doors of the church anymore. Choosing to go to church, especially for younger people, is a countercultural option. The United States has become a new mission field, and we really do not know how to be missionaries.

꜠ ꜠ ꜠ ꜠ ꜠ ꜠ ꜠

These changes are only the front edge of the tsunami of change that has swept over American church culture in the last forty or so years. Given all this, it should be no surprise that many of us feel anxious. The world has changed, and the changes seem to be out of our control. We don't know what to expect or in which direction to move. How does the church navigate such change?

This is a book about churches operating, under the power of God's Spirit, as Sailboats run under the power of the wind. It reflects my passionate belief that God has more in store for the church than we have known. These resources are gifts of the Holy Spirit that Jesus promised to the first Christians and still gives to those today who are willing to put down the oars and put up the sails. The things I am writing about here are not new. I did not invent them; they come from Scripture. Neither does this book contain a "ten easy steps" plan for how to grow your church. Rather, I call the church to walk an ancient path that will open us up to the power of God for our time.

This book is built around the image of the church as a Sailboat. This boat has sails spread wide, allowing the wind of the Spirit to move the church where God wants it to go. It is God-powered. The Sailboat image is a metaphor. A metaphor uses an image to point beyond itself. For instance, "You are my sunshine" is a way of saying that a person is absolutely important in your life. That person is not sunshine in the sense of being particles of light that come from the sun. But he or she is *your* sunshine. Likewise, the church is not literally a sailboat. But it can choose to operate in a way that allows the Holy Spirit—the wind of God—to become its power source.

In his poem "Footnote to All Prayers," C. S. Lewis refers to "our limping metaphors."[1] All metaphors have their limits, and this one is no exception. I know that I will be bumping up against the limits of the Sailboat metaphor from time to time. I apologize for it in advance. Also I apologize to real sailors everywhere who find I have not dealt properly or in depth with the technicalities of sailing. In spite of its flaws, I do believe that this image, with its invitation to drop the oars and put up the sails, carries the possibility of a new future for many Christians and congregations today.

Spiritual truth generally comes to us in seed form, and whether or not the seed bears fruit depends to a large degree on how we nurture it. I have included in this book reflection/discussion questions to help you in the nurturing process. My prayer is that groups of church members will read and discuss *Sailboat Church* together, praying for God to help them raise the sails and navigate God's church into God's future. It is still true that God "by the power at work within us is able to accomplish abundantly far more than all we could ever ask or imagine" (Eph 3:20).

Chapter 1

# Created to Sail

*E*arly Christian symbols include a boat as a symbol for the church. In Jesus' time, there were two ways to power a boat on open water. One was to use muscles, most commonly by rowing. The other way was to harness the power of the wind. When the early Christians used a boat as a symbol for the church, it was never a rowboat; it was always a sailboat. That is because on the day of Pentecost, with "a sound like the rush of a violent wind" (Acts 2:1), Jesus' promise of power became a reality and drew those who believed in him into a different way of living.

For these early Christians, church was a God-powered, God-led, God-resourced adventure. They found they were caught up in something much bigger than themselves. Day by day, hour by hour, they moved as the Holy Spirit led them. They depended on the Spirit to provide what was needed to do God's work. They knew that God was really in charge of what was happening. On Pentecost, they received the gift of spiritual resources to participate with Jesus in his transformation of the world. As they felt the wind of the Spirit begin to blow around them that day, they raised their sails and began the process of learning how to become sailors.

The essential difference between rowboat and Sailboat churches may not be apparent on the surface. Both kinds of churches may be active and growing in numbers. Both may struggle and even die. Whether a church is liberal, conservative, or middle-of-the-road is no indication of whether it is a Sailboat or a rowboat. They both exist in urban, suburban, and rural areas. The difference is in the attitude of the members and leaders.

## Rowing the Church

The bedrock reality of life in the rowboat church is that "God has given us a basic agenda (for example, to make the world a better place, save souls, help the poor, spread Christian truth, and uphold justice) and then left it up to us to get on with it." The dominant attitude in this congregation is either "*We* can do this," or "*We* can't do this." The church focuses on circumstances, such as the money it has or can raise, the available volunteers, the charisma and skill of the leaders, and the demographics of its community. The rowboat congregation believes and acts as if its progress depends on its own strength, wisdom, and resources. It's all about how hard, long, and well people are willing to row.

In his book *Let Your Life Speak,* Parker Palmer writes about "functional atheism, the belief that ultimate responsibility for everything rests on us. This is the unconscious, unexamined conviction that if anything decent is going to happen here, we are the ones who must make it happen—a conviction held even by people who talk a good game about God."[1] Functional atheism is at the heart of rowboat mentality. It offers intellectual assent to the idea that God is sovereign over creation, while usually acting as if what we do determines the outcome. If, in our deepest hearts, we really believe we are pretty much left alone in the universe to fend for ourselves, our congregations will tend to act like just one more human institution. In the worst case, a church is reduced to a religious do-it-yourself project focused on making the world a better place or on helping people cope or on any number of other worthy but secondary goals.

The distorted idea that the church is basically a human religious organization tends to creep into minds and hearts unconsciously over time. In spite of speaking about God quite a bit, studying a book that claims to be God's word, and doing activities we believe God wants us to do, the actual experience of the personal presence of God is not much sought or expected in the church or in the lives of its members. Eventually worship grows cold. Teaching becomes distanced from God's call on our lives. The congregation has little impact on the world outside its buildings. Intimate spiritual fellowship turns into surface socializing. Lives are not transformed; neither are communities.

In rowboat congregations, spiritual realities are effectively discounted. In this way of thinking, only things that can be seen, heard, felt, and counted make a substantive difference. To act as though material circumstances have the last word on us or on the church or on the world effectively discounts God's sovereignty and puts us at the mercy of whatever our circumstances may be. This version of functional atheism leads us to a life of impotence amid the powers and principalities of this world.

Another indication that we have forgotten our sails and taken up rowing is the frantic search for ways to fix perceived problems of both congregations and denominations. This need-to-fix mentality often manifests as a craving for a programmatic or organizational magic bullet. We seek a "how-to" strategy that will cause problems to disappear, making us the successful church we desperately want to be. Millions of dollars have been spent on books, conferences, and programs offering a simple fix for sinking churches. As good as some of these programs may be, they generally do not engage people at the spiritual depth required for permanent change in a healthy direction.

Another form the urge to fix takes is finding the right person to put in leadership. Here, someone, usually a staff person, is seen as the answer to the congregation's problems. Pastors especially are often judged by whether or not they can "fix" the church. If a church is failing, members often assume that it is the pastor's fault and that if they had a new one, things would be better. While leadership is a key piece of the transformation puzzle, few people have the level of charisma and skill required to revive a plateaued or dying church through personal effort alone. And even if they could, experience indicates that when that person retires or moves on to the next place, the church often loses energy and members as it reverts to old patterns of behavior. Getting the "right preacher" is no guarantee that the church will move out of dysfunction and decline, certainly not for the long haul.

Another form that trying to fix the church takes is looking beyond the congregation to place blame: "If only so-and-so were different we could grow." Each person holding this view fills in the "so-and-so" according to his or her personal views. For instance, there are those who think that if their denomination's policies and pronouncements were different, the congregation would be more successful.

Much energy is spent to manipulate the policies of various church bodies to this end. When the conflict level becomes too great, such congregations may seek to change their affiliation as a way to fix the problem.

All these ways of fixing the church have in common the underlying assumption that we human beings have the ability to do what will make the ultimate difference. The conviction that our decisions, our wisdom, our planning, our hard work, our right theology will make all the difference is a lightly disguised form of works righteousness. God is the only one who saves. However, the idea that we can and should fix the church, a first cousin to the heresy of salvation by works, is widely found in rowboat congregations.

Rowboat churches also tend to act as if what happens in the church buildings *is* church. It is a common assumption among North American Christians that *church* means an organized institution that meets in certain buildings on certain days and times. If a church is successful and thriving, those buildings will be full of people on those days and at those times. Money given by the people who come to church will be invested in keeping up the buildings and providing programs that take place in them. A successful church also has professional staff members who are charged with providing services and programs for people who are members of the church. Staff members also must make sure that enough money is donated to keep the buildings open, the staff paid, the programs going, the services happening, and the organization growing in membership. According to this line of thinking, the test of a church's vitality is mainly what staff makes happen in the church buildings.

Rowboat churches often tend toward a mind-set of scarcity, which hampers many in their mission and ministry. They tend to look at what they have in the way of resources, and then base plans for ministry and mission activities on those resources. When the resources run out or run low, the churches give up or go into a survival mode. They pull back to the minimum and stretch the limited resources as far as they can to survive for as long as they can. When a rowboat church runs out of resources, that's the end.

All these characteristics of rowboat churches can be traced back to faulty conceptions about the nature of the church and the nature of God. If we believe that God has left us alone to do the work of the church by ourselves, we will row. Rowing also flows logically from believing that the church is essentially a human religious institution, with all the limitations that being human carries with it.


## Sailing the Church

In contrast, the bedrock reality of life in the Sailboat church is that God "through the power at work within us can do abundantly far more than we could ever ask or imagine" (Eph. 3:21). Sailboat churches tend to focus not on their own situation, resources, or limitations but rather on discerning God's unfolding will. They engage in intimate partnership with God, trusting God to provide and do what only God can do. These congregations live in the creative tension between two spiritual realities.

The first of these realities we hear from Jesus at the Last Supper with his disciples: "Without me you can do nothing" (John 15:5). *Nothing* is a very harsh word. It must have been hard for the first disciples to hear Jesus talk about his going away from them, and then to hear him say, "Without me you can do nothing." How was God's agenda going to be accomplished if Jesus was going away and if without him they could do nothing?

*Nothing* is still a hard word for believers to hear today. Yet Jesus also says to twenty-first century Christians: "Without me you can do nothing." Without me, he says, you can give religious speeches, but you can't preach the gospel. You can hold church services, but you can't worship. You can put biblical and theological informa-tion in people's minds, but they won't come to faith. Without me, it is impossible to do my ministry or accomplish my mission. This sounds offensive to our ears because at the top of just about any human list of virtues is a can-do spirit. Deep down, we feel "it's all up to us." Most Christians today would agree, at least in theory, that doing God's work should somehow involve God, but in practice, God tends to be a distant or even absent partner.

As we have seen, in a rowboat church, as long as the church is able to keep rowing, people are often reluctant to do anything else. Row-ing means that we are in control; we are getting the job done. When we reach the point where we can't row any more or when rowing is not getting us where we need to go, then we are faced with a choice. One option is to give up. Some congregations simply run out of people or money or energy and close the doors. Others take what they have and just spread it thinner and thinner until it runs out. Another very sad outcome is that congregations turn inward and begin to fight each other until conflict finally tears the church apart.

Other congregations in a similar situation, decide to try doing church in a new way and begin to sail. Sailboat congregations know that they cannot make the wind blow, but they do realize that they can tap into spiritual resources beyond themselves by reorienting their efforts and catching the wind of the Spirit. This brings us to the second reality that Sailboat congregations live by. We hear it in the angel Gabriel's response to Mary's question, "I am a virgin. How can I bear a child?" Gabriel's response is elegantly simple: "With God nothing is impossible" (see Luke 1:35–37).

Sailboat churches know that when God becomes the chief guide and power source in their lives and ministries, the unthinkable moves into the realm of the possible. Jesus' disciples thought his story was finished when they put his dead body in a tomb and rolled a stone across the door, but God had other possibilities in mind. Just as human will did not produce Jesus, neither did human power have the last word on his life. He came to bring a new reign of God on the earth, which nothing could ever equal or destroy. The church was created to announce and demonstrate this new creation and to be a staging ground for partnering with God in saving the world. Only congregations that are living into a transforming relationship with this God for whom nothing is impossible can hope to fulfill their potential as the body of Christ.

Rowers are confined to the power they can generate themselves; sailors learn to let the boundless power of the wind move them where they need to go. Sailors live in the creative tension between our weakness and God's power, between our poverty and the wealth of resources God provides to those who obediently seek to do God's will. Living between the realities of "without me you can do nothing" and "with God all things are possible" is both humbling and exciting. We are constantly reminded that we are powerless to do the work of Jesus' church without him. At the same time, we find that the wind of Christ's Spirit still blows in the world, and as we put up the sails God does amazing things.

## Questions for Reflection

1. How do you react to the idea of our life together in the church as an adventure with God? How do you see your church experiencing this adventure?
2. What do you think Jesus meant when he said: "The one who believes in me will also do the things that I do, and, in fact, will do greater works than these, because I am going to the Father" (John 14:12)? How do you think the first disciples felt when they heard this promise?
3. How have you experienced the reality that God both calls and provides what is needed to fulfill the call?
4. What difference would it make in your life if you took very seriously these words of Jesus: "Without me you can do nothing"?

Chapter 2

# The Sailing Life

*I*n real life, no congregation will function like a rowboat or a Sailboat all the time. Most churches will experience a mixture of sailing and rowing. But if God is calling us to do more sailing than rowing, then it is important to be able to recognize what this might look like in church life. This chapter will explore some attitudes and practices that tend to cluster around sailing.

*Sailboat churches experience church as a divine-human partnership.*

Anyone who has ever sailed knows that, in its own way, sailing is just as much work as rowing. Sailing, however, requires a different kind of activity. Sailors put up and shift the sails and partner with the wind to move the boat. In the Sailboat church, God and believers work together as partners. In this partnership what we do is important; what God does is essential.

Church sailors know that the essence of church is participating in a dynamic, interactive process with a living God. Therefore, they are suspicious of one-size-fits-all plans for making the church into what it should be. There is no precise map for the journey, rather the details unfold as we are drawn into the adventure. The wind blows where it will and takes us with it. The important thing is to be faithful and obedient in response to what God seems to be doing. As we do this, the way forward will be revealed.

*Sailboat churches make nurturing relationship with Jesus Christ a top priority.*

Right before Jesus told his disciples, "apart from me you can do nothing," he said, "I am the vine, you are the branches. Those who abide in me and I in them bear much fruit" (John 15:5). Everything flows from the relationship. Leaders in Sailboat congregations believe helping people grow as active Christ followers is the first priority. They keep Jesus at the center of the church's life and its mission. No amount of work, skill, money, intelligence or charm can take the place of the *abiding* relationship with the Lord and head of the church. As this relationship develops, Christ will lead us, through his living Spirit, into the work we are to do and provide what we need to do it.

If we are not abiding in Christ, the value of our most successful efforts at church work or mission are called into question. The work of God and a relationship with God must go together. Jesus makes this clear in the Sermon on the Mount. Speaking of the judgment day, he says, "Not everyone who says to me 'Lord, Lord' will enter the kingdom of heaven, but only the one who does the will of my Father in heaven. On that day many will say to me, 'Lord, Lord, did we not prophecy in your name, and cast out demons in your name, and do many deeds of power in your name?' Then I will declare to them, 'I never knew you; go away from me you evil doers'" (Matt. 7:21–23). For Christians, knowing God and doing God's will are tightly bound up together. If we are not about doing God's will, then something is wrong with the relationship. If the relationship is what it should be, then we will be engaged in doing God's will rather than our own.

All deep relationships involve paying attention to the other. The experience of knowing God is no exception, and our commitment to that relationship requires that we spend time and energy investing in its growth. Sailboat congregations engage in intentional practices, communal and individual, that foster more powerful relationships with God. They create spaces and opportunities in church life for people to experience God's presence and hear God's call. Worship in a Sailboat congregation is a passionate engagement with a real and present God. All this deepens the divine-human partnership that is at the heart of a Sailboat church and helps the church both bear and be good news beyond its doors.

*Sailboat churches are Holy Spirit powered.*

Just as there is no sailing without the wind, so there is no church worthy of the name apart from the Holy Spirit. The lethargy of many congregations today can be traced directly to ignorance of or apathy toward the third person of the Trinity. Left to our own devices, humans default toward creating religious do-it-yourself projects instead of being the body of Christ and doing God's will. These projects may be satisfying to varying degrees, but they do not bear lasting fruit for God's kingdom.

We are not capable of being the body of Christ in the world without the active, empowering work of the Holy Spirit. This is the way it was meant to be from the beginning. Jesus was Spirit-powered and Spirit-directed in everything he did. Christians, singly and together, are meant to live like him. Sailboat churches know this and are always seeking a deeper, obedient intimacy with the Spirit of God. As we move into this reality, we are called to repent of things that grieve the Spirit. We let go of personal agendas in order to let the Spirit move us into participating in God's agenda. And we learn to trust the Spirit to supply what we need to participate in God's mission.

*Sailboat churches live by prayer.*

How do we come to know and be known by God? How do we, in this world, participate in the life of the risen Christ through his Spirit? Scripture testifies that we do so through prayer. God has chosen prayer as a major means by which the power of the Spirit flows into the world. Jesus spoke of this relationship over and over again, often in extravagant terms. "So I say to you, Ask, and it will be given you; search and you will find; knock and the door will be opened for you. For everyone who asks receives, and everyone who searches finds, and for everyone who knocks, the door will be opened. . . . If you then who are evil, know how to give good gifts to your children, how much more will the heavenly Father give the Holy Spirit to those who ask him" (Luke 11:9–10, 13)!

When we pray, we invite God's graceful power into our lives, the church, and the world. Prayer gives the Spirit "place and space" to work in our lives. When we do not pray, much that God wants to do in us and through us is stymied. Sailboat congregations do not necessarily understand prayer. Much about prayer is beyond human understanding. However, they do pray fervently, persistently, and hopefully.

*Sailboat churches are shaped and guided by interaction with Scripture.*

Just as Christ is the living word of God, so is Scripture the written word of God. This revelation has been given to us by God so that we will know who God is, what God requires of us, and what God is up to in the world. Sailboat congregations know that in order to engage in God's mission in the world they need to be formed by God's written word. This ongoing process of formation keep us centered on God and what God wants instead of on ourselves and what we want.

Militating against this process of formation is the reality of a high level of biblical illiteracy in most congregations. People have to actually read and study Scripture before it can begin to shape them. This process of formation, however, goes far beyond simply collecting biblical knowledge or being able to quote Scripture by heart. The Bible begins to shape and form us when we ask the Holy Spirit to speak to us through this ancient book. Sailboat congregations interact with Scripture as a living thing. Scripture speaks and demands changes in thinking and behavior. It not only gives us knowledge but also challenges us, convicts us, encourages us, comforts us, and at times makes us very uncomfortable. Experiencing this relationship with Scripture requires a different approach to Bible study than what many churches offer. Often it requires not only individual study but also engaging with other people in an intimate community listening together as Scripture forms and guides our lives. Sailboat congregations find ways to open up creative space where people, both individually and in groups, can hear God's voice speaking directly to them from the Scripture.

*Sailboat churches require spiritual leaders.*

Spiritual leaders are people who help others to seek and do God's will. They are passionate about God and live toward the goal of having God firmly seated at the center of their lives and of their church. They want God to be the one who shapes their desires, their decisions, and their actions. They have a lively relationship with a God, who is always doing a new thing. This is the heartbeat of sailing congregations.

These spiritual leaders, both clergy and laity, know that any authority they bear is delegated to them by Jesus. They know better than to lead by doing what seems right in their own eyes. Rather they look to him through his Spirit to set the course, enable them to navigate, and provide the resources they need to keep sailing. Without this kind of Spirit-attuned leadership, it is unlikely that any church will sail.

Anyone who has ever served in the Navy can tell you that the captain rules. Sailors look to the captain to set the course and guide the ship's passage. The captain delegates authority to others on the ship, but there is no doubt who is the final authority. In a Sailboat church everyone, especially the leaders, know who their captain is; and it's not the pastor, the governing board, or the most influential member of the congregation. Jesus Christ is the Lord and head of the church. His atoning death on the cross brought us back into right relationship with God. His Holy Spirit birthed the church on Pentecost. Without Jesus there would be no church. He is the captain of our lives and of our congregations. Sailboat congregations must have leaders who understand this and who lead by being led by their Lord.

*Sailboat churches take spiritual realities and resources seriously.*

We do live in a material world. However Sailboat congregations know that spiritual realities are just as real as material ones. God is a force to be reckoned with. God has the ability (and the will) to influence people and things to fulfill divine purposes. Sailboat churches know that no earthly lack or circumstance can tie the hands of God. The adventures of Sailboat churches often push them beyond the wisdom, money, and abilities they have. That does not stop them. If a congregation is doing mission in such a way that it is never challenged beyond its own resources, it is probably rowing instead of sailing. In the Sailboat church, as people pray and act in faith, the Holy Spirit draws forth the resources necessary for them to do what God truly wants them to do. The God who calls is the God who provides.

*Sailboat churches live to sail.*

In marinas all around the world there are boats that seldom leave the dock. They remain tied up there, perhaps used as places to entertain or relax, even to live on, but their sails are rarely raised. They hardly ever engage the wind in the partnership of sailing. So it is with many churches. They have beautiful buildings, run programs that are of educational and therapeutic value to the people who attend, and may engage in a variety of good works. However they seldom cast off, raise the sails, and allow the Holy Spirit to move them away from the dock and out into the world.

In contrast, Sailboat churches know that they exist to sail with the winds of the Spirit on the course that God has set out for them in the world. The members of these churches also understand that God has called each one of them into the sailing life. This is how it was meant to be from the beginning. The earliest Christian congregations knew they existed to sail. Their main business went on out in the world. Their gatherings were for the purpose of learning how to be followers of Jesus in daily life. When they gathered they received spiritual nourishment and support for that calling, and they worshiped the God who had saved them, gathered them, and was accompanying them on the adventure. For them, the life of the believing community in fellowship with Christ *was* church. Wherever they went, they were the church because he was with them.

What institutional structure the church had in those days—and being human requires some means of organization—was simply to help the church carry out its mission of being and making disciples in the world.[1] It is sad that institutional considerations such as membership, buildings, and budgets have come to play such an important role in defining the church today. Christian sailors know that these institutional forms are not essential. They are meant to function like the dock at the marina. The dock and what happens there are important, but sailing is the point. In Sailboat congregations, the buildings, structures, budgets, and programs are seen not as ends in themselves, but only as means to an end. They can be changed or jettisoned if they get in the way of sailing.

*Sailboat churches are places of transformation.*

Living close to Jesus through the Holy Spirit changes us. In a Sailboat church, people grow out of the need to be the center of their own universe, becoming less self-centered and more God-centered. This growth enables a Christ-like quality of life to flourish in the body and creates a community of believers who bear the fruit of the Spirit. Paul says this fruit is "love, joy, peace, patience, kindness, generosity, faithfulness, gentleness, and self-control" (Gal. 5:22). As we bear this fruit of the Spirit, our life together in the church shows evidence of the abundant life only God can give. The world has nothing to compare with it. This Spirit-life is a powerful form of witness to the seeker and the unbeliever.

True abiding with Christ also leads us into the world to partner with the Holy Spirit in doing God's transforming work there. Sometimes we do this as part of the congregation's mission. Other times we may do it as individuals in our neighborhood, our places of business, or through volunteer or civic work in the community. This holy partnership can have a powerful transforming impact on people, families, and communities beyond what we will ever know this side of heaven.

*Sailboat churches teach and practice discernment.*

God is always calling us into a new future. We also hear other voices calling us in different directions. Christian discernment is about sorting out God's voice from the others and making decisions based on the desire to be in the flow of God's will. It also involves a commitment to do God's will whatever it may be. God is not inclined to reveal his will to those with only an idle curiosity or academic interest in it. As a friend noted, "In my own life I have observed that when I follow through on what I perceive as the nudges of the Spirit, the nudges seem to continue. And when I don't follow through, over time I find myself feeling out of the stream of the Spirit."[2] While all believers benefit from practicing discernment in our individual lives, Sailboat churches teach and practice communal discernment. This is a prayer-saturated process in which a body of believers allows the Holy Spirit to lead them into discovering and doing God's will. Along with a commitment to obedience, it involves making space and taking time to listen to God and to one another, reflecting on options in light of God's call and our desire to be faithful, and making decisions in the light we are given, trusting that God will honor our obedience and redeem our mistakes. The practice of discernment is formative. Sailboat congregations discover that coming at decisions in this way shapes them into being like Jesus and helps them be Jesus-like in their life together.

## Questions for Reflection

1. How do you experience yourself as a partner with God in God's work in the world?
2. How do you see your church partnering with God?
3. How do you experience your church being the body of Christ outside the church buildings?
4. What part does prayer play in the life of your congregation? In your own life?
5. Think of the last time you had a big decision to make. How did you go about making it? What part did God play in the decision and how you went about making it?
6. When do you experience your church sailing?

Chapter 3

# The Wind

$E$arly Christians used the image of a Sailboat with sails billowing in the wind to express their experience of church. This image casts believers in the role of sailors partnering with God's Holy Spirit to go where God wants us to go and do what God wants us to do. To live fully into this divine-human partnership we need to know more about the Spirit.

Many Christians would say that they believe in the Holy Spirit—after all the Spirit (also known as the Holy Ghost) figures prominently in the Apostles' Creed—but when pushed, they will admit that they relate more easily to the Father and the Son than to the Spirit. Many of us really have a duality in our faith instead of a Trinity. Jesus and the One he called "*Abba,*" Father, are real to us, but the Holy Spirit is a foggy enigma. This chapter will try to clear up some of that fog so that we can understand more about our sailing partner.

The first thing we need to say is that the Holy Spirit is a *who* instead of a *what*. Christian theology talks about the Spirit as a person, specifically as the third person of the Trinity. For many of us, this just complicates an already difficult concept by adding another on top of it. But calling the Spirit a person and part of the Trinity does clarify a few things, one being that the Spirit is living and personal. Even though we use the image of the wind to talk about the Spirit, in reality the Holy Spirit is not an impersonal force of nature. The Spirit is as much a living, personal being as are Jesus and God the Creator. "The Spirit is not a magical 'something' that gets into us but *Someone* who comes to dwell in and among us."[1] The best place to learn about this Someone is in Scripture.

## The Spirit in the Beginning

The Bible tells us that the Holy Spirit was present before the world was created. Genesis reports that the *ruach* (Hebrew word translated into English as wind, breath, or spirit) from God swept over the watery chaos before the world began. As creation progresses, Adam is created, and the *rauch* from God goes into Adam to bring him to life (Gen. 2:7). Along with participating in creation, the Spirit of God also sustains everything that is. This is a moment-to-moment act of God's grace; God's *ruach* in us keeps death at bay. Wherever there is life instead of death in the world, God's sustaining Spirit is at work and has been since the beginning.[2]

In the Hebrew Scripture, God's Spirit was said to "come upon" people to fit them in special ways for God's work. For instance, Judges 3:10 reports that in a time when Israel was under attack, the Spirit of the Lord came upon Caleb's younger brother, and he led Israel. The Spirit also equipped him for war against Israel's enemies. Mostly, however, the Spirit sent prophets to tell God's people to repent from their rebellion and idolatry.

There were also prophets of Israel who pointed toward a day when God's Spirit would be more widely distributed among the people. Joel prophesied that on that day the Spirit would be poured out on young and old, men and women, even on male and female slaves (Joel 2:28). This amazing gift of God's Spirit was to be one outcome of the healing of Israel's relationship with God. Jesus came to bring about this healing.

## Jesus and the Spirit

The Holy Spirit is intimately woven throughout the whole of Jesus' life and ministry. In announcing Jesus' conception to his mother, the angel Gabriel points to the work of the Spirit. He tells Mary that the birth of her child—Israel's long-awaited Messiah—will happen when "the Holy Spirit will come upon you and the power of the Most High will overshadow you" (Luke 1:35). Luke ends Gabriel's visit to Mary with words that point to the things the Spirit will bring about in the years ahead: "For nothing will be impossible with God" (v. 37).

At Jesus' baptism, shortly before his ministry begins, we hear that "just as he came up from the water, suddenly the heavens were opened to him and he saw the Spirit of God descending like a dove and alighting on him" (Matt. 3:16). The power and authority of Jesus came from being the Son of God, full of the Holy Spirit. The Spirit enabled him to speak, heal, teach, cast out demons, raise the dead. These miracles and others astounded people and showed that Jesus had power beyond what their own religious leaders possessed (see Matt. 7:28–29). Jesus did everything in his earthly ministry through the power of the Holy Spirit who filled him to the brim.

The Holy Spirit is the spirit of Jesus. To be filled by this Spirit means that we will become more like Jesus. We will live as he did, doing God's work in the world, because we will be like him through his Spirit's presence in us. We cannot be effective disciples of Jesus without welcoming the Spirit who empowered Jesus' own ministry. Being filled with the Spirit is meant to be a constant, ongoing process for every Christian.

Jesus gave the Spirit to the church as a gift to transform us and fit us for ministry. In his farewell address to the first disciples, Jesus says, "If you love me, you will keep my commandments. And I will ask my Father, and he will give you another Advocate, to be with you forever. This is the Spirit of truth" (John 14:15–17). Doing Jesus' work without his Spirit is impossible.

## Community in the Spirit

On Pentecost, the pouring out of the Holy Spirit created a new kind of community. It was a body of people who were to participate with God in the salvation of the world. By their lives and actions, they were to show the reality of God's rule in this world and the world to come. The risen Christ was present with them through his Spirit, giving what they needed to do God's work.

Much of what the New Testament has to say about the Holy Spirit is about the life of God's people together in the church. In the fourteenth through sixteenth chapters of John's Gospel, when Jesus talked about the coming and work of the Spirit, he consistently used the plural pronoun "you" (or "you all" as we say where I live.) What

Jesus says is aimed at the disciples—soon to be church—*as a group*. The thrust here, for instance, is not "you individually will bear much fruit" but rather "you, the church, will bear much fruit" (John 15:5). Still today the presence and power of the Spirit is given, not primarily for the enjoyment and use of individuals; rather, the Spirit is given to build up the church for its shared mission (1 Cor. 12:7).

This giving of the Spirit to the church is the beginning of something much bigger than we usually envision. It is not just about getting people right with God or making sure they are going to heaven when they die. The pouring out of God's Spirit on disciples is a major move in God's plan to save the whole creation and make it new. "God has promised that through his Spirit, he will remake the creation so that it becomes what it is straining and yearning to be . . . a world set right. . . . The work of the Spirit in the lives of individuals in the present time is designed to be . . . a down payment and guarantee, as it were, of that eventual setting to rights of all things."[3] When this plan is completed, God's will shall be done on earth as it is in heaven.

Through the presence and power of the Spirit, we believers have a major role to play in creation's transformation. Our ability to participate with God in this plan is absolutely contingent on the presence of the Spirit in and among us. Without the Spirit moving and acting in power, the church devolves from the living body of Christ into a well-intentioned but generally impotent religious organization.

## The Spirit's Work in the Church

How does the Spirit operate to bring a new kind of life to the church and to its members? First of all, John's Gospel says that the Holy Spirit is "the Spirit of truth" (John 14:17). "Truth" here does not refer to truth in a general sense, but rather to God's truth, particularly the truth about our sin, God's salvation, and the divine plan for saving our world. If we are able to come to saving faith in Jesus Christ, it is because the Spirit has moved in our minds and hearts so that we are grasped by God's redeeming truth.

As we grow in our ability to receive this truth, the Holy Spirit gives us glimpses of things as God sees them and as God wants them to be. The Spirit enables us to see beyond the blinders of culture, custom, and self-interest to catch a vision of the world around us from God's perspective. Scripture is our main source for understanding God's truth. The Spirit works in our minds and hearts as we read and interpret Scripture individually and together. We begin to understand how God's eternal truth can take shape in our time and our situation and to see what faithfulness requires of us.

For example, Jesus commissioned his disciples to go out into the world and to make disciples of all nations. The book of Acts tells us the story of how the first disciples lived out this commission in their first-century world. But what does it look like when twenty-first-century believers attempt to be faithful to that commission? And how is God calling our particular congregations to be disciples and to make disciples in our communities and to the ends of the earth? Each church is called to see its community through God's eyes and catch a vision of what God wants it to be doing. Without the Spirit giving us "eyes to see," we will be blind to God's will. Later on I will explore this movement of the Spirit in the church under the heading "Practice Sanctified Imagination" (see p. 67).

*The Spirit is our teacher.*

Jesus says that "the Advocate, the Holy Spirit, whom the Father will send in my name, will teach you everything, and remind you of all that I have said to you" (John 14:26). The Spirit brings to our memory what Jesus taught and did and helps us make connections with our own situations. So often when we are faced with difficult things, our minds become fixed on the problem to the extent that we become distracted and discouraged. The Spirit works to bring to our memory treasures of the faith that can encourage us and help us stay focused on God and God's will.

The teaching of the Holy Spirit is not just about ideas and concepts. The Spirit also leads us into new patterns of behavior and new ways to make decisions. Under the influence of the teaching Spirit, we learn to be different and do things differently. Our lives are more and more oriented to God as our true north, and we are able to resist the lies and temptations that can draw us away from God's agenda. In the church, the Spirit teaches us to discern where God is calling and how to make decisions based on that call rather than on considerations of institutional success/survival or maintaining congregational comfort.

*The Holy Spirit is our Advocate and gives us peace.*

Jesus said to his disciples on the night he was betrayed, "I will not leave you orphaned." . . . "I will ask the Father and he will give you another Advocate, to be with you forever" (John 14:18, 16–17). The Greek word translated into English here as *advocate* or *helper* carries the image of someone standing with another person in a court of law or some other threatening situation. The idea is that the circumstances require more than we can provide for ourselves. We need someone with power to accompany us and to work on our behalf.

Whenever believers in Christ are called into challenging situations, the Holy Spirit stands beside us to support us. We are never alone or without resources. We do not have to let anxiety and worry dominate our lives. For example, Jesus made this promise to disciples called to give account of their faith in time of trial: "Do not worry beforehand about what you are to say; but say whatever is given to you at that time, for it is not you who speak, but the Holy Spirit" (Mark 13:11). The Advocate will supply the very words we need to make a faithful witness.

Through this Advocate, Jesus also gives us peace beyond anything the world can give. The peace that the world gives is a fragile thing built on a foundation of favorable circumstances, plentiful resources, success, and good fortune. The peace that the Holy Spirit brings to believers, however, flourishes in the hardscrabble soil of struggle, danger, weakness, and lack. This peace is built on the foundation of trust and hope in God, who never forsakes the believer. As the Holy Spirit gives us this peace, we are empowered to take risks of faith for God's sake that those who see only with worldly eyes will never understand. Peace comes not because we are strong but because the Holy Spirit enables us to believe that God is strong.

*The Holy Spirit is the source of power for the believing community.*

When many Christians think about the Holy Spirit, the charismatic movement comes to mind. It burst on the religious landscape of the United States most recently in the 1960s, when its practitioners sought to bring the gifts of the Holy Spirit to the center of the

Christian experience. This movement energized some people and terrorized others. For decades, stories abounded of church members or sometimes ministers attending charismatic conferences and coming back to split their congregations apart. A number of churches paid dearly in those days for the spiritual immaturity of people on both sides of the charismatic fence. In some circles, the shadows of fanaticism and schism hung for decades over anything deemed to be "spiritual." The very words "Holy Spirit" became suspect.

The root of the word *charismatic* is found in the Greek word *charis* or "gift." The main focus of the charismatic movement was on the gifts of the Spirit, especially the flamboyant gifts and manifestations of the Spirit, such as speaking in tongues. This focus on gifts often created a sense among other Christians that charismatics thought of themselves as spiritually elite. With good reason, persons not caught up in the movement resented the implication that their faith was lacking if they were not speaking in tongues and having knock-your-socks-off emotional experiences. This focus on gifts created a have and have-not division in the church.

For the church to be equipped by the Spirit for the mission of our day, a different approach seems in order. Rather than focusing on *charisms* or gifts it might be more helpful to focus on *dunamis,* that is power. *Dunamis* is the word used in Acts when Jesus tells the disciples that after they receive power, they will be his witnesses in Jerusalem, in Judea, Samaria, and to the ends of the earth (Acts 1:8).

Power is sadly lacking in many of our churches today, spiritual power that transforms lives and has a major impact on communities and the wider world. When you really think about it, this *dumanis* of the Spirit is the only thing the early church had going for it. Its members had very little of this world's resources. However, the Spirit's power of the risen Christ that was poured out on all believers at Pentecost gave them everything they needed to do God's will. The Spirit did for them what they could not do by or for themselves.

This is the spiritual power of the obedient, crucified Lamb of God who still calls us to deny self, take up our crosses, and follow in his footsteps. It comes to the church as we put aside our agendas and let God move to the center of our common life. This power can transform us in ways beyond what the therapist, doctor, or social worker can offer. It enables us to engage the powers and structures of this world and turn them toward the reign of God. Ultimately this is the power of God that will transform the kingdoms of this world into the kingdom of our Lord and of his Christ.

God's power changes things we cannot change and provides resources beyond what we have ourselves to do God's work. The Spirit can draw us together when, left to our own devices, we will remain divided. When every path seems blocked, the Spirit can show us God's way forward. The Spirit opens doors that to human strength remain stubbornly closed. Minds are changed and hard hearts softened not by our human arguments but by the power of the Holy Spirit. Spiritual gifts to fit us for God's work come from the Spirit. These things are only a small part of what the Holy Spirit can do in the church. When we know that the One who empowered and equipped the first disciples is eager to do the same for us today, we are set free to live for God with joyous abandon.

## Questions for Reflection

1. If asked to come up with a description of the Holy Spirit in five words or less, what would you say?
2. Read Acts 1–2. Make a list of what these passages say about the Holy Spirit and what the Spirit does. How does this help you understand the Spirit better? Or does it raise more questions?
3. The Holy Spirit is the power of God to do for us what we cannot do for ourselves. Have you experienced this in your life? In your church?
4. Does the peace that God gives differ from being happy? In what ways? Reflect on a time when you had a peace that was beyond all understanding?
5. Have you ever encountered the charismatic movement? If so, how has that encounter shaped your understanding of and relationship with the Holy Spirit.

Chapter 4

# Our Boat, the Church

## The Body of Christ

*T*here is no other organization on the face of the earth exactly like the church of Jesus Christ. The early church struggled for centuries to clarify who Jesus was, finally expressing its conclusions in AD 381 in what we know as the Nicene Creed. In it, they declared that Jesus is "true God from true God, begotten, not made, of one Being with the Father," yet they say he also "became truly human."[1] The great paradox of the incarnation is that Jesus is both 100 percent divine and 100 percent human, all at the same time.

The church, as Christ's body, also is both divine and human. As a divine, God-ordained movement, it is holy because it is created and powered by God. Jesus Christ promises to make himself known in the world through the church. God, not human beings, created the church. Because of this, the church is more than an organization of people who enjoy getting together to do religious exercises and good works. The church is a divine, even supernatural, community gathered by God to do God's work.

It is important to keep all this in mind because the church's divine nature is not always easy to see. Sometimes it takes great faith to believe that the church as we know it is the body of Christ. Sin is all too evident in our midst. But the church was never meant to be a group of holy people who are *in themselves* morally superior to everyone else. Remember that the apostle Peter denied his Lord three times, yet Jesus forgave Peter and commissioned him to "feed my sheep" (John 21:15–17). From its very beginning, the church has been a community of sinners daily seeking forgiveness and new life through Jesus Christ.

The holiness of the body of Christ does not come from its individual members. It comes from Christ, who keeps us in grace and gives forgiveness, transformation, and new life. The apostle Paul goes so far as to say that the very human frailty and imperfection of the church serves to glorify God: "We have this treasure in clay jars [KJV has "earthen vessels"], so that it may be made clear that this extraordinary power belongs to God and not to us" (2 Cor. 4:7). There *is* a divine treasure in the body of Christ, and it is contained in the earthen vessel of human frailty and imperfection. When good things happen in and through the church, it will be obvious to everyone that they must come from God because earthen vessels cannot produce these results.

Scripture does not say, "Someday you will be the body of Christ," or "If you try hard, you might get to be the body of Christ," or "If you reach certain levels of perfection you could be the body of Christ." The statement is absolute: "Now you are the body of Christ and individually members of it" (1 Cor. 12:27). This is true in spite of all the weaknesses and sins to be found in church leaders and members. Spiritual sailors learn to keep sight of the church's divine nature in the midst of its human imperfections as they do God's work in the Sailboat church.

Now we will explore how and why the church came into being.

## In the Beginning, God

In the beginning, there was no church. There was only God. Humans were created to live in loving, obedient relationship with God. It was to be our joy and privilege to commune with God intimately in the midst of a creation where everything was ruled by God's good purposes. In some mysterious way, this communion also seems to be the linchpin of creation. When that relationship broke down, as we see in Genesis 3, everything that God originally made good was infected with brokenness. Obsession with self became the default mode for human beings. God's desires for the creation were pushed to the margins of life.

However, God did not give up on humanity or the world. Instead, the Creator went to work to make the world right again. One of the first steps toward this goal involved the calling of an ordinary, elderly couple named Abram and Sarai. They were chosen to partner with God in the blessing of "all the families of the earth" (Gen. 12:3). This calling was also an invitation to a new way of life. Abram and Sarai were not to be self-centered any longer. Rather God was to be at the center of their lives—calling, guiding, and providing—much as it was with Adam and Eve in the beginning. Through the miraculous birth of a son to this aged couple (now renamed Abraham and Sarah), God created a people called Israel. It was from these people many years later that the Savior of the world would come. The roots of the church are planted deep within the ground of God's covenant promises to Israel.

Unfortunately, the chosen people found living God's way as much a struggle as Adam and Eve did. The idea that a good life was possible apart from loving, depending on, and obeying God continued to drag down the human race. In addition to this, powers of evil at work in the world took every opportunity to lead people away from God. Even people who wanted to live God-centered lives often found themselves doing just the opposite.

## In the Fullness of Time, Jesus

In spite of this sad history, God never gave up on the people of Israel or on the dream of a healed creation. In the fullness of time, God, in the person of Jesus, came to earth to do for us what we human beings could not do for ourselves. Not only did his teaching give people a transforming vision of what God wanted for them and for the world, but Jesus himself was also God-in-action among them. He was God embodied, and he had a specific mission. Jesus came to take back God's world from the evil that human disobedience had unleashed. Everything about Jesus—including his death and resurrection—happened so that people would be saved and reunited in loving partnership with God, and so that the creation would be healed.

Jesus could have done everything he was called to do by himself. Instead, as God did with Abraham and Sarah, he invited ordinary human beings, disciples, to be his partners in doing God's work. Their first job was simply to be with Jesus, listening and learning as they went with him through the towns and countryside. Being with Jesus brought them into contact with an energy and authority they had never seen before. His touch, his words, his presence were full of God's power.

To be with Jesus was to experience a new quality of life. It was real human life in every way, and yet it was also filled with an energy that could come only from God. Jesus referred to it as being "born from above" (John 3:7). Before long the disciples began to sense that Jesus was not just another rabbi but that he was God's own "anointed one" who could really make the world right again.

Unfortunately, their ideas about what that would look like and how to make it happen were not the same as those of Jesus. They expected him to lead a movement to throw the Roman invaders out of their country and to set up God's rule by force. They believed in the power of the sword, but Jesus showed them another kind of power. This power carried him through a crooked trial, through torture and crucifixion, even through feeling abandoned by God. Though it looked to those watching like the worst kind of defeat, Jesus' faithful obedience even unto death brought with it the power to remake the world.

Long before his death, Jesus made it clear that he *did* expect his disciples to take an active part in his ministry. The Gospel writers report in various ways that Jesus sent them out and gave them spiritual authority to do signs and wonders and to call people into the new thing that God was doing on the earth. Then at the last supper, he told them, "Very truly, I tell you, the one who believes in me will do the works I do and, in fact, will do greater works than these, because I am going to the Father" (John 14:12).

In his suffering-servant death on the cross, Jesus gave birth to the church. He is the captain of our Sailboat. His cross is its mast. He calls believers to live as sailors, setting sail by the Spirit and navigating in the flow of God's will. But even if the sails are raised and the sailors are ready, a Sailboat has to have wind in order to sail. This is why what happened on Pentecost is so crucial to the church's story.

## On Pentecost, the Spirit

The first chapter of the Acts of the Apostles tells us that after Jesus was taken out of the believers' sight, they went back to Jerusalem and waited for his promise to be fulfilled. As they waited, they did several significant things. First, they continued the practice of getting together. This group of people had little in common except their experience of Jesus—living, dead, and resurrected. Nonetheless, as they kept getting together their experience of Jesus unified them, his living presence strengthened them, and they were able to claim his promises for their common future.

These times of gathering were occasions for prayer. As the disciples waited for the promised power, they "were constantly devoting themselves to prayer, together with certain women, including Mary the mother of Jesus, as well as his brothers" (Acts. 1:14). Perhaps they remembered Jesus saying, "If you then, who are evil, know how to give good gifts to your children, how much more will your heavenly Father give the Holy Spirit to those who ask him?" (Luke 11:13). It was on this expectant, praying group that the Spirit came in power on Pentecost.

The book of Acts is the story of how God used their obedient faithfulness to do amazing things. From Pentecost day onward, the Holy Spirit worked within the first believers to help them understand the true meaning of Jesus' life, teachings, death, and resurrection. The Spirit drew together a diverse group of men and women into a strong, unified community. It empowered the preaching of the believers and accompanied that power with signs and wonders pointing to God's gracious salvation. Through the power of the Holy Spirit, the believers discerned God's will and found courage when they ran afoul of political and religious authorities. The Advocate that Jesus had promised did for them what they could not do for themselves and, before long, blew them out of Jerusalem to change the world forever. And they did it, not with their own wealth, wisdom, and power but through participating with the Holy Spirit in Jesus' resurrection life and power.

The church was created to be a Spirit-powered mission movement, and in this regard nothing has changed since the day of Pentecost.

Looking at the existence of many churches today, one might think that a new design for the church was given later. In some cases, this new design seems to have omitted God's mission altogether. These churches exist to serve the personal religious and social needs of their members. They have minimal presence outside the walls of their buildings. Using our boat metaphor, they are not even rowboats. Rather they function like pleasure barges tied up permanently at the marina. This way of being church is not pleasing to God. In the book of Revelation, we hear Jesus speaking to a church like this: "I know your works; you are neither cold nor hot. I wish you were either cold or hot. So because you are lukewarm, and neither cold or hot, I am about to spit you out of my mouth" (Rev. 3:15–16).

Other churches, which do understand that God expects them to do something beyond meeting their own needs also miss the mark and end up as rowboats. Their mission design involves little prayer, discernment, listening for the Spirit, or dependence on God to direct and provide. Instead, without centering their efforts in these God-honoring practices, rowboat churches come up with projects that seem good to them and carry them out with the resources at their disposal. They settle for what they can do in their own power. These efforts at mission may seem successful on the surface. However, because they do not involve a partnership with God, they bear little lasting fruit for God's reign in the world. As Jesus said, "Without me, you can do nothing" (John 15:5).

One of the ways we end up rowing is to read the accounts of the Spirit-powered first believers and assume "That was then, and this is now. They had resources at their disposal we don't need or can't have. What they experienced was for their particular time in history. God gave them special gifts to get the church off the ground. Now that we are well established, we don't need that kind of thing." This kind of thinking cuts us off from experiencing the power of the Spirit for our day. Scripture teaches that the resources of Jesus, his Abba, and the Holy Spirit are just as available to us now as they were to the early church! We can sail as they did, or we can choose to keep rowing.

In the next chapter, we will look at what the church is supposed to be doing in the power of the Holy Spirit.

## Questions for Reflection

1. When have you seen the church acting like the body of Christ?
2. What attitudes and practices tend to keep churches tied to the meta-phorical dock in the marina?
3. Why do you think God created the world?
4. How do you see the love of self as the default mode for humanity being played out in the world?
5. What proportion of your congregation's money and energy is spent meeting the needs of its members? What proportion is spent in mission beyond the congregation?

Chapter 5

# The Church's Mission

$S$ailboat churches live to partner with the Holy Spirit in what God wants to do for the world. This is our mission. In so doing we follow Jesus, who lived to do the work of "the one who sent me" (John 4:34). Involvement in mission is also the way the church finds its continuing life and vitality. Every church, no matter how large or small, has a part to play in God's work for the sake of the world.

In one sense, each congregation's call to mission is unique because no congregation is exactly like any other. Even two churches of equal size and resources on opposite sides of the same street corner may be engaged in mission in different ways. What is really important is that each congregation discerns how God wants to partner with it and then works with God to carry out that call. This said, there are still some things that the church is to be about in every age and place. As your congregation prays and discerns the shape of its own particular partnership in God's work, here are some avenues of mission to pray about.

## Proclaim the Good News

Jesus came to take God's world back from the powers of evil and death. By his own death and resurrection he won the victory against evil forever. Jesus made it possible for human beings to live as children of God's light. Through the Spirit and the church, God is at work right now to set right everything that went wrong when our first parents chose a life apart from God. Church is the place where people believe this good news and worship the One who made it possible. Church is also the place where this good news is preserved, celebrated, taught, and preached, and from which it is broadcast to all the world.

Every other facet of our mission is founded on the fact that the church and its members have good news to share. First Peter 2:9 tells us that the church is "a chosen race, a royal priesthood, a holy nation, God's own people, in order that you may proclaim the mighty acts of him who called you out of darkness into his marvelous light." Other organizations do good things that resemble other forms of the church mission, but proclaiming God's saving love and power to the world is uniquely the mission of the church.

## Demonstrate God's Reign

Usually we think about mission as something that happens outside the church. But this facet of the church's mission has to do with the life of the church itself. An important part of the purpose of the church is to be a place where people can experience something of God's reign in the world right now. We are called to relate to one another differently than the world does. At its best, the quality of life in Christian congregations is a little taste of what is to come in the fullness of time when Christ makes all things new. We see a picture of this kind of community in the second chapter of Acts.

> They devoted themselves to the apostles' teaching and fellowship, to the breaking of bread and the prayers.
>
> Awe came upon everyone, because many wonders and signs were being done by the apostles. All who believed were together and had all things in common; they would sell their possessions and goods and distribute the proceeds to all, as any had need. Day by day, as they spent much time together in the temple, they broke bread at home [note: Or "from house to house"] and ate their food with glad and generous hearts, praising God and having the good-will of all the people. And day by day the Lord added to their number those who were being saved. (Acts 2:42–47)

Clarence Jordan, founder of the Koinonia community, spoke of the church as providing a "demonstration plot" for the kingdom of God. He borrowed this term from agriculture. A farmer wanting to use new seed, plants, fertilizers, or insecticides can first try it out on a small patch of ground. This demonstration plot lets the farmer see firsthand the results of the new product. Jordan used this term to talk about the Koinonia Community, which he founded in south Georgia in 1942. Koinonia was intended to be a place where people could see what it looked like when believers took God's directions for life seriously. They based their community life on the account of the early church in Acts 2 and following chapters. In Jordan's particular demonstration plot of the kingdom, believers were invited to live together as an extended family. They pooled their personal financial resources for the use of the community, and they refused to participate in racial segregation. The way of life of the Koinonia community did demonstrate powerfully the new kinds of relationships God intends for the church. It had a life-changing effect on many, especially young people.

There is no one template for every church's witness to God's plan for the world, and not every church is called to the path the Koinonia community followed. However, every congregation is called to be, in its own way, a demonstration plot of God's kingdom on this earth. As such, the common life of each congregation will bear the fruit of the Spirit in ways people can experience. The presence of hospitality, forgiveness, kindness, generosity, joy, patience, love in the church should be evident to members and nonmembers alike.

Having set this as our goal, still we must confess that human effort cannot produce the fruit of the Spirit. No matter how good our intentions, without God's life-giving presence we will tend to default to doing what feels good to us. We will settle for being friendly to one another and letting strangers fend for themselves. We will tend to hold grudges and nurse hurts that build walls between believers. We will default to the natural human tendency to hold on to what we have instead of acting out the truth that everything we have is God's. The fruit of the Spirit is produced only when the Spirit of Christ is active in the congregation and people are intentionally committed to growing in discipleship to Jesus. It is the responsibility of a congregation's leaders to guide the church in a continual process of self-examination, confession, and renewal. Along with the leaders, all members must be alert to opportunities for the church to be more Christ-like. Everything about the church's life should reflect the goodness, healing, forgiveness, and justice of God.

Sailing with the Spirit not only produces certain kinds of actions but also, and perhaps primarily, makes us a certain kind of people who live together in a Christ-like community. Living in the Spirit means that, in our own ways and situations, we begin to live into what God intends the world to be like. Our way of life demonstrates God's intention for the future of creation to the world. This brings us to another facet of the church's mission—inviting others to participate with us in God's future.

## Invite People into Relationship with God

Jesus came to invite all people into a new way of being with God. This relationship made an immediate and eternal difference in the lives of those who answered his call. The early Christians were clear that discipleship included inviting others in to what they had experienced through Christ. They were especially known for inviting the poor, widows and orphans, sick people, and slaves into their fellowship. Knowing Jesus meant making him known to others, no matter who they were.

Sharing the good news and inviting people to abundant life in God is still a core function of the church. While many other organizations do good works in the world, it is the unique function of the church to point to Jesus Christ as the savior of the world and invite people into relationship with him. No amount of philanthropic action takes away this responsibility. However, sometimes invitation is not simple or easy.

Many of us have come into contact with Christians who tried to evangelize us or others in ways that were abusive or condemning. Sometimes what passes for sharing the good news feels more like manipulation or coercion. At the same time, the prevailing rule of the culture around us is that faith is a personal matter and should be kept private. How can we break through all this and communicate our faith in ways that are faithful, that invite rather than repulse?

I suggest a model from Scripture. In John's Gospel, we find Jesus engaging in conversation about God with a woman of Samaria. He made such an impression on this woman that she went home and called the people of her town to "Come and see a man who told me everything I have ever done! He cannot be the Messiah, can he?" (John 4:29). This woman does not brow beat people or condemn them. Neither does she have answers to all the theological questions people may be asking. She simply invites people to "come and see" what she has experienced in her encounter with Jesus. This come-and-see approach to faith sharing takes it out of the theoretical and brings it down to where we live. The Christian church is a community where people sing, "I once was lost, but now I'm found, / was blind but now I see."[1] What we share with others is what God has done for us.

Inviting others into what God is doing in the world and what God can do for them draws us into close partnership with the Spirit of God. Unless God is at work in our lives in real and visible ways, we will have little reason to say, "Come and see!" Without the Spirit opening the hearts and minds of people, our inviting will go nowhere. We cannot save anyone or argue them into Christian faith. Instead, our mission is simply to invite others to "come and see what God has done!" As our lives and words give evidence about how God is transforming us, God will use our witness to draw others into new life.

## Engage in Loving Service

When Jesus' disciples were fighting over which of them was the most important, Jesus said, "the greatest among you must become like the youngest, and the leader like one who serves. . . . I am among you as one who serves" (Luke 22:26–27). Jesus spent much of his time caring for the needs of others. He fed the hungry, healed the sick, calmed storms, cast out demons, and brought the deranged back into their right minds. He did all these things out of compassion. Jesus was human. He felt all the sorrows and pains of being human. He could feel like and for us because he was one of us. He responded by doing things to help, heal, and encourage.

Along with his human compassion, Jesus also had God's heart for the world. Scripture says that Jesus came to earth because God loved the world (John 3:16). Everything he did reflected this divine love. He came to serve the world because he loved us and the whole creation in spite of our sin. He did what was best for us even while we were crucifying him.

Faithful disciples of Jesus will not ignore the needs of people around them. Neither will they hide from the problems of the world. Being transformed into disciples means that Jesus himself will draw us into contact with those we are meant to serve. The Spirit will bring people our way who need loving service. As this happens it is important to remember that the way in which we interact with these people is as important as what we do for them. We can hand someone a sack of groceries and wish them a good day. However, as we do this over and over again, our charity can become toxic and the results of our service can become destructive to the people we are trying to help.[2]

It is challenging to listen deeply to people in need and engage in honest relationships that encourage accountability, dignity, and healing. As we do this more and more, our own resources will not be sufficient for the task. We will find that rowing will not get us where we need to go when we move beyond superficial charity to sacrificial service. In these deep waters, we must lay down the oars and put up the sails.

## Offer Prophetic Witness

A fourth facet of our mission as disciples of Jesus is to bring the judgment and gospel of God to bear on the structures and culture of our time. As the prophets of old sought to speak the word of God to the evils of their day, so is God's church today called to speak God's word to the evils that confront us. Prophetic witness and action that grows out of it seek to bring God's truth and God's ways to bear on the world in which we live.

Sometimes this kind of mission grows out of loving service. As Christians become involved in helping people, it is natural that they should also become concerned about the causes of the problems they are seeking to remedy. Feeding hungry people may lead a congregation to grapple with the problem of unemployment and then with deeper economic issues. Helping refugees may draw us into deeper issues of immigration, economics, or foreign policy.

This movement from particular problems to larger issues frequently raises questions about the church's right to speak on so-called secular matters. These things are often controversial and may spark conflict in the church when members have differing opinions. In spite of this, we cannot claim to be faithful in God's mission if we are not faithful in the public arena. The lordship of Christ extends not only to individuals but also to societies.

This is because the gospel has a forward thrust, and it carries the whole world toward the final coming of God's reign. If Jesus is Lord of all the earth, then it is appropriate that we share with him in moving this world closer to what God wants it to be. This task immediately brings us into contact with social and political structures. It may involve defending these structures when good ones are threatened. It may take the shape of speaking out against and working to change those we believe to be contrary to God's will. Either way the church is called to do what we can, individually and collectively, to make a difference for God in the world.

The great problems of our day—hunger, violence, racism, poverty, and terrorism, among others—may seem insurmountable. The reformation of the world and the work to bring its values more into line with the intentions of God is not a task we can accomplish by human effort alone. The powers of darkness are too great for us. Again, we find that we are pushed to move beyond rowing to sailing. Challenging the powers and principalities of this world requires us to move obediently in the power of the Spirit, using God's resources and following God's direction to do God's work in this world.

## Questions for Reflection

1. How do you experience the church as the body of Christ, a good demonstration of what God wants for the world?
2. Think about the last time you visited a church where you were a stranger. How were you received? Would you have wanted to join that church? Why or why not?

3. How does your congregation deal with people who come to the church asking for help? Do you know the names of any of these people or their situations?
4. Has your church ever been led to speak or act publicly on a controversial issue? If so, what was the effect of your witness?
5. Where in your congregational life do you find the church moving beyond rowing to sailing?

Chapter 6

# The Making of Sailors

*C*hurches are made up of members, and in order for the church to sail with the wind of the Spirit, its members must be willing to be sailors. This is not to discount the importance of leadership in determining the character of a congregation. Leaders usually spark the changes necessary for a church to lay down the oars and raise the sails. However, no matter how committed and excited the leaders are, if a critical mass of the church's members do not identify as sailors and practice the moves of sailing, that congregation will probably end up rowing into the future. This chapter will look at some basics involved in being a sailor.

## Trust Jesus

People join or remain in churches for many reasons. For example, there are social reasons: "It's where my friends are." Sometimes people want to be part of a group doing good things in the community. Others were born into the church and continue out of habit or duty. Still others involve the family in church because they want their children to have a moral compass. None of these reasons are bad, but they are not what the church is really about.

The core purpose of the church is to partner with the Holy Trinity in the salvation and re-creation of the world. Christian sailors are people who intentionally commit to this mission and put themselves under the authority of the Lord and head of the church, Jesus Christ. This kind of commitment is not about building up a human religious institution. You don't sign on to sail in Jesus' navy to pump up church programs or to increase giving or to recruit more members. Christian sailing is a way of life that involves a committed, personal relationship with Jesus Christ. We sail because Jesus calls us to be sailors.

Faith and trust in Jesus are at the heart of the sailing church. Sailors trust that what happened through Jesus' life, death, and resurrection has eternally bridged the gap between God and human beings that resulted from human rebellion against God. They trust this not only in a general or intellectual way but also particularly, personally for themselves. Trusting Jesus also involves inviting him to take control of our lives. This is what we mean when we say, "Jesus is my Savior and Lord."

We make this internal movement of trust because we know we need something we cannot do for ourselves. We cannot fix ourselves, and we cannot fix the world. Trusting Jesus is about trusting that God has already set in process all the fixing that needs to happen for us and the creation. We are invited to be part of something that is already going on in the world through the power and grace of God. When we accept this invitation, we intentionally become part of what Scripture calls the kingdom of God or the kingdom of Heaven. There is a real eternal shift in the orientation of our lives. We have been called "out of darkness into his marvelous light" (1 Pet. 2:9).

As we come into a trusting relationship with Jesus, we learn that everything that could ever separate us from God or condemn the world to eternal darkness is being wiped away. This trust makes a life and death difference. "You were once dead through trespasses and sins in which you once lived, following the course of this world, following the ruler of the power of the air, the spirit that is now at work among those who are disobedient. . . . But God, who is rich in mercy, out of the great love with which he loved us even when we were dead through our trespasses, made us alive together with Christ" (Eph. 2:1–5). Being awakened from death into life is not just about our eternal destination or the quality of our inner lives. It is a shift from being self-defined to being defined by the call and purposes of Jesus who gives us this new life.

So we are Christian sailors because something has happened and is happening to us. Jesus Christ has called us personally from death into life. Jesus has moved beyond being a historical figure, a religious great teacher, or a moral mentor for us. He has become the person to whom we owe our lives and everything we hope for in this world and beyond. Jesus has called us into relationship with him, and this relationship is central to who we are. We may be toddling along in this relationship. We may have our doubts and questions about it all. We may stray from it regularly. However, as sailors we have intentionally chosen to trust Jesus as the one who gives truly abundant life now and into eternity.

How do we come to this relationship of trust? Scripture is very clear that we cannot do it by the force of our will or even by our strongest desire. As God at the cross did what was necessary to redeem us and the world, so God is the prime mover whenever anyone comes to love and trust Jesus. If we feel desire for this kind of relationship, the Holy Spirit is already at work in us to that end. Without the Spirit's presence and work, we would have no such desire.

The way into this relationship is to pray our desire. Such a prayer might go something like this:

> God I know that I need you. I also know that there are mountains between us that I cannot climb over or move. I cannot make myself believe in you. Neither can I fix the most basic problems in my life. I need you to do what only you can do. I trust (or I want to trust, or I want to want to trust) that Jesus can bring me over everything that separates us. I want him to do this, and I invite his Holy Spirit into my life to take control so this can happen. Make me able to trust that this work is happening in me day by day in spite of how I feel or anything else. Protect me from any attempts to destroy my faith or push me back to where I started. I pray this trusting not in myself but in what Jesus did for me out of love. So be it.

## Become a Disciple

If a relationship of trust with Jesus is the first step into being Christian sailors, becoming a disciple is step two. In the first century, students gathered around teachers called *rabbis*. These students were known as *disciples*. Rabbis taught their disciples to interpret the Torah, the books of Moses. But they also taught them how to live as faithful Jews. Being a disciple was as much a matter of identity as intellect. It was understood that the disciple meant not only to learn what the rabbi knew but also to become like the rabbi. Becoming a disciple was a personal commitment to adopt the teacher as a model for faithful living. To this end, disciples not only studied with their teacher but also often lived together as a community in the rabbi's home or followed him as he traveled around the countryside.

Jesus was one of these traveling rabbis. All four Gospels tell stories about Jesus and his disciples. Jesus deliberately chose not to be a lone-ranger type of leader. He gathered people around him and invited them to be part of what he was doing for God. He called men and women to follow him, and they often left their families and jobs to do so, walking miles on foot through Galilee and Judea. These disciples gave up life as they had known it and gave themselves to being with Jesus. He became not only their teacher but also the center of their lives. The parables about the pearl of great price and the treasure hidden in a field (see Matt. 13:44–45) reflect the experience of these first disciples. In him, they found something so good that it was worth giving up everything else to get it.

Jesus came announcing to people that the kingdom of God had arrived and called his disciples to live into it. This kingdom, or reign of God, occurs when God's will is done on earth as it is in heaven. The Sermon on the Mount gives us a sense of what life looks like when we live under God's reign. In his life and teachings, Jesus embodied this gracious, loving reign of God for all to see. He did things that only God could do. In very real and practical ways he broke through the powers of evil that ground people down and separated them from God. He created a new way of life governed by the culture of heaven. His healings and miracles were signs and tastes of God's will for the world. Jesus taught people about the new world that was coming into being, but beyond teaching, he invited them to live in it by trusting him and becoming his disciples. And so it still is today.

No one can be an effective sailor without first being a disciple of Jesus Christ. Intellectual agreement with a set of truths about Jesus is not discipleship. Discipleship is about identity with him and commitment to his way of life. This is a place where many Christians have gone badly wrong. Knowing who Jesus is plays a part in learning to love, trust, and obey him; but that is only the beginning. Right believing is not an end in itself. It is meant to lead us into a dynamic, empowering relationship with God through Jesus in the power of the Holy Spirit.

In his farewell address to his disciples in John's Gospel, Jesus speaks of the relationship he wants to have with his disciples as *abiding*: "Abide in me as I abide in you. Just as the branch cannot bear fruit by itself unless it abides in the vine, neither can you unless you abide in me. I am the vine, you are the branches. Those who abide in me and I in them bear much fruit, because apart from me you can do nothing" (John 15:4–5). Being a disciple is about the abiding life. The relationship that Jesus and disciples have is meant to be as intimate and life-giving as that between a vine and its branches. Everything else depends on this.

It is important to remember that we do not create the abiding connection. It is a gift from God. When we trust Jesus and allow him to have control of our lives, he moves in and takes up residence with us through the Holy Spirit. Neither can we keep abiding in our own strength. Our part in abiding is to remain in communion with him and depend on him for everything. Depending and receiving are key; we came into the relationship by grace, and we can stay in it only by grace. Jesus warned his first disciples, "Truly I tell you, unless you change and become like little children, you will never enter the kingdom of heaven" (Matt. 18:3).

The key universal characteristic of children is that they are dependent. Many would-be sailors miss the boat because they are not willing to be completely dependent on God. They want to do God's work in their ways through their own power and resources. Jesus shows us what obedient abiding looks like in his relationship with the one he called *Abba*. Their abiding in each other produced the salvation of the world. In the same way, our ever-increasing intimacy and dependence on Jesus bears the fruit of God's will in us, in the church, and in the creation.

## Be Filled with the Spirit

One consequence of trusting Christ and abiding with him as a disciple is that the Holy Spirit takes up residence in us. In the upper-room speech in John's Gospel, Jesus tells his disciples that they will do the works that he does and even greater works "because I am going to the Father" (John 14:12). Going to the Father points toward what will happen when Jesus is no longer on earth with them in body. At that point, the Spirit will be poured out upon and into the disciples. They will know the Spirit "because he abides with you and he will be in you" (John 14:17).

Receiving the Holy Spirit into themselves transformed the first disciples. On the night Jesus was betrayed to his death, all the disciples ran away and left him. After Pentecost, members of this same group stood in front of the court that sent Jesus to the cross and roundly refused to obey the court's order not to speak about him. Before Pentecost, the disciples were weak and tentative in their faith. After Pentecost, they witnessed passionately and emphatically about Jesus at every opportunity. The disciples were divided and jockeying for position even at the Last Supper. After being filled with the Spirit, they were "of one heart and soul" (Acts 4:32). The Holy Spirit enabled them to find a way through their differences for the sake of the church's mission. The church was able to withstand every kind of persecution and still flourish because the Spirit that gave Jesus victory over the cross was living in them.

This same Holy Spirit is still available to disciples today, and receiving the Spirit into ourselves is an essential component of the sailing life. How can the Spirit be both in us and outside of us filling the sails of the church? Think of it this way—the same air we breathe into our lungs is also moving all around us in the world. Remember that the Hebrew word *ruach* is translated as "wind," "breath," and "spirit." So while the Spirit abides in us, the Spirit is also at work in all kinds of ways beyond us in the world. Things happen that we do not expect and can hardly imagine when the Spirit starts to fill us and move around us and in the church.

As we think about being filled with the Spirit, it is important to remember that we do not control or own the Spirit of God in any way. Indeed it is just the opposite. When the Spirit fills us, we are possessed by God and full of God. So instead of saying "she or he has the Spirit," we should really say "The Spirit has him or her!" And this possession or filling is not a one-time thing. As the writer to the Ephesians urges the believers there to live up to their calling, he says "do not get drunk with wine, for that is debauchery; but be filled with the Spirit" (Eph. 5:18). The verb tense here implies "keep on being filled with the Spirit" or "be continually filled by the Spirit." The idea is that this filling is a process that goes on all the time as we need the Spirit to live as effective and faithful disciples of Jesus Christ.

A good help in understanding this continual filling is the story of the manna in Exodus 16. The manna came every day according to God's promise, and it was supposed to be gathered daily except on the Sabbath. Gathering more manna than was needed for the day was forbidden. When people tried to store up enough manna for more than one day, it rotted. Short-term but continuing provision seems to be the way God operates. Prayer for the Spirit to fill us and equip us for the day keeps us grounded in our dependence on God. It keeps us in relationship. This is what God wants above all else.

## Put on the Whole Armor of God

Christian sailors are called to "live as children of the light" (Eph. 5:8) in a world that often denies God's light and seeks to subvert it. The writer of Ephesians warns his community that they will face resistance because "we do not wrestle against flesh and blood, but against the rulers, against the authorities, against the cosmic powers over this present darkness, against the spiritual forces of evil in heavenly places" (Eph. 6:12). In other words, there are forces not immediately evident to us that are at work to defeat Christ's purposes in this world and to subvert our discipleship. Jesus alluded often to the resistance believers would experience as they took his good news out into the world and tried to live by it (see, for example, Matt. 5:11). However, he also assured them that the church was founded on solid ground and "the gates of Hades will not prevail against it" (Matt. 16:18).

How are we to equip ourselves for this challenging calling? We know that we cannot stand against these forces of evil in our own strength. Human powers are no match for the "cosmic powers over this present darkness" (Eph. 6:12). Instead, the writer of Ephesians urges believers to "put on the whole armor of God, so that you may be able to stand against the wiles of the devil" (Eph. 6:11).[1] Armor is protective clothing. The armor of God will not keep us from experiencing hardships. Instead we can trust that as we wear it, God's purposes for us cannot be defeated. The epistle to the Ephesians describes this armor in rather cryptic phrases. Many commentators have tried to parse out exactly what each piece of the metaphorical armor refers to, and their varying conclusions can be confusing. Instead, I would suggest that the passage as a whole refers to spiritual practices that protect us as we seek to resist this present darkness.

The first practice is that of keeping Jesus—the way, the truth, and the life—front and center in our lives. Out of all the claims on us in this world, his come first. This means taking time to remember regularly that he saved us and made us worthy for fellowship with God. It means meditating on the cost of this and the love it shows. As we do this we are grasped by the truth that we are people of value, regardless of our earthly condition or status, because he gave his life for us. We also remember how he is working in our lives each day to heal us and enable us to fulfill our calling as children of the light. Remembering and meditating on these things leads us to worship and praise God for what we have received. There is a holy cycle of remembering and worshiping that keeps us focused, not on the circumstances around us that would pull us down, but rather on God who delivers us. Participating intentionally, daily, in this focus on Christ, the truth armors our mind against the Adversary.

The second practice we are to put on as armor is the practice of right living. Our essential calling as Christians is to live in such a way that God's will is done on earth as it is in heaven. People should be able to see the light of Christ shine through our presence and our behavior every day. This calling brings with it certain ethical and moral challenges. We are called to be noticeably different from those who walk in the moral murk of this present darkness. We are to live by the teaching and in the Spirit of Jesus, our very lives shining with grace and goodness. In particular, we are to proclaim the "gospel of peace" (Eph. 6:15) with our actions and in our relationships. The heart of this piece of armor is setting our will to desire God's will. Here, prayer is key. We cannot put on the armor of right living by our own strength. It has to be placed on us by the Holy Spirit, and that happens through constant prayer.

Third is the practice of faith. Faith means keeping our eye on God in the midst of all the things that would drive us to sin or despair. In putting on this piece of armor, feelings can be our most challenging enemy. Faith is not how we feel about God or life or our circumstances or other people. To have faith means that we turn our focus away from these things to remember the power and promises of God for us. Faith means that "we, by an act of will, must turn from our affinity, or bondage, to the rebellion and the dominion of darkness and deliberately embrace Jesus as the true Lord of all."[2]

Many people feel like failures at faith because they cannot get away from their doubts. This is an insurmountable problem if faith is understood as a mental process. If faith is the ability to believe in something and never question, then few of us would be able to have faith. It is much more helpful to think of faith as a posture or practice than a mental attitude. Faith is the practice of always turning toward God as flowers turn toward the sun. In the posture of faith, we are constantly reorienting ourselves away from feelings and problems toward the promises of Scripture, the face of Jesus, and the power of the Spirit.

A wonderful picture of faith is found in the story of Paul and Silas in prison. Arrested for disturbing the peace by performing an exorcism, they were stripped, beaten, and put in stocks for the night. Rather than bemoaning their fate or railing against the injustice of their arrest, the story says that at midnight they were praying and singing hymns to God (Acts 16:16–40). That is faith in action! Faith looks beyond feelings or circumstances to claim the reality of God's sovereignty in the world and in our lives. Those who are constantly practicing faith by the power of the Holy Spirit ignite a light that cannot be put out.

A fourth practice that armors us against attacks of the Adversary is remembering that we have a God who saves. Ephesians talks about this as the helmet of salvation. From the very beginning, as soon as our first parents chose to live a half-life apart from their creator, God began to work for the salvation of creation and the human race. The Bible is a story of a saving God re-creating a broken world. Saturating ourselves with this story through Scripture rescues us from two kinds of despair.

The first kind is personal despair about ourselves and those we love. No matter how much is wrong in our lives, we are children of the light. This identity is not of our making. It comes entirely from God and does not depend on our ability to understand it or fully live up to it. It has to do with what Jesus has done for us, not what we can do by ourselves. To trust Jesus is to become a child of the light. Nothing can take this away from us. And beyond ourselves, because the grace of God is so powerful and because God loves to save, we should have a strong hope for the salvation of all people.

Grasping that God is about the work of salvation also keeps us from the second kind of despair, despair about our world. One of the great hymns of the church pleads "Save us from weak resignation to the evils we deplore."[3] Weak resignation is one of the wiles of the Adversary. It grows from feeling that the problems are so big and our resources are so small that nothing we do makes a difference. This way of thinking binds us in apathy and keeps us from playing our part in the great drama of the world's salvation. The apostle Paul urged the believers in Rome, "Do not be conformed to this world, but be transformed by the renewing of your minds, so that you may discern what is the will of God—what is good and acceptable and perfect" (Rom. 12:2). Constantly reminding ourselves that God is in the process of saving the world energizes us to look for places where this salvation is taking place and join in. This is our mission as children of the light!

The fifth and final practice that armors us for confrontation with our Adversary is appropriating the power of God's word for our lives and mission. Scripture is powerful. Many of us have felt that power while singing songs or hymns, hearing a sermon, or participating in a Bible study. Confrontations with Scripture can transform us through our thinking and behavior. Every Christian is responsible to put on this piece of armor through the reading and study of the Bible. When we engage in Bible study individually or in small groups, we put ourselves where God has promised to meet us. Reading and meditating on Scripture is a means of grace for our lives.

Just reading Scripture or even studying it is not enough, however. We must let Scripture work on us so that we are shaped into the people God means us to be. The writer of Ephesians calls the word of God a sword. It gets under the surface of our lives, cutting down to where we really live. It confronts us with God's demands on our life. It challenges us with demands beyond our own strength and drives us to our knees in prayer to God.

I think of this approach to the Bible as "marinating" in Scripture. Cooks marinate food so that it is filled with the flavor of what it soaks in. Marinating in Scripture, being fully open to its power, transforms us more and more into the image of Christ. It makes us people who not only hear the word but also do it. In this way we grow as children of the light, becoming living testimonies of what God is about in the world.

This chapter has explored some basic elements of what it means to be a Christian sailor. The next chapter will look at ways sailors work together raising the sails so that the Holy Spirit can carry the Sailboat church where God wants it to go.

## Questions for Reflection

1. Most of us have a number of ties that bind us to a particular church. What are some of the ones that keep you in your congregation? Have your motivations for being a member changed over the years?
2. Try to put into words the essential purpose of the church. In what ways does your congregation fulfill this essential purpose?
3. How do you hear Jesus saying, "Come, follow me" in your life?
4. How has your relationship with God changed over the years?
5. Think of someone you would call "a child of the light." Describe what it is about that person that makes him or her such a blessed child.

Chapter 7

# From Rowboat to Sailboat: Raising the Sails

*I*t is much easier to build a Sailboat church from scratch than it is to convert a rowboat church into a Sailboat. Some of the most exciting new congregations around are those that intentionally planned from the beginning to sail, to be God-powered and Spirit-led. This kind of new church naturally attracts people who want to sail. As the congregation grows, its members learn together better and better how to put up the sails and move with the wind. Sailing becomes the culture of the congregation.

These congregations are fairly rare. Many churches have been operating largely in the rowboat mode for decades. The mast is still there, but the sails are seldom raised. With oar locks bolted into place, the members have calluses from rowing. What about these churches? Can a rowboat become a Sailboat? The answer to that question comes to us from the mouth of Jesus. "For mortals it is impossible, but not for God; for God all things are possible" (Mark 10:27). By God's grace any church can sail, and any Christian can learn to be a sailor. If the idea of Sailboat church appeals to you, perhaps the Holy Spirit is calling you and your congregation into an adventure with God. If so, what's next?

First, we can't row our way into sailing. We may embrace the biblical vision of the Sailboat church. We may passionately want to see our congregation sailing. We may be willing to give up the rowing life for the joy of sailing. However, the power to turn rowboat into Sailboat does not lie with us. Only God can do it. We must keep in mind that this is not about fixing the church; rather it is about letting God once again be our true north and our power source. God leads each congregation by the hand in the way that suits its own situation.

It is an intimate, interactive journey that no program or plan can shortcut. What follows are some of the postures and practices that act as spiritual sails. As we raise these sails, the Holy Spirit fills our common life, transforms us, and moves us where God wants us to go.

## Prayer, the Mainsail

If you want to know whether a congregation is living as a Sailboat or a rowboat, ask about its practice of prayer. Prayer saturates the lives of leaders and members in a Sailboat church. It is deeply and broadly woven into the church's culture. More than anything else, prayer serves to make life in the Sailboat church a transforming experience for individuals and communities.

Prayer is vital to Sailboat churches because these congregations are not content with what they can do with their own resources, wisdom, and strength. Through prayer, they find that God supplies them with what they need to do much more. This experience of God's abundance and miracles shapes the congregation's vision and expectations. Over time, God uses this investment in prayer to draw them deeper into his will, making them more like Jesus through the power of his Spirit. As this process unfolds, such congregations find prayer becomes increasingly central to their life and mission.

God has chosen prayer as the main way God's power flows from heaven to earth. However, this kind of prayer is not about telling God what to do. Neither is it about making deposits in a spiritual bank account so that when we reach a certain level God does what we want. There is no guarantee that if we pray enough or in the "right" way, things will go our way. We do not give God orders; rather we hold hands out to receive what God wants to do in and through us.

Along with being a source of power, prayer is a means of relating with the God we know in Jesus through the power of the Spirit. Prayer is about intimate relationship, and this kind of relationship always transforms. In prayer we acknowledge our dependence on God and our need for what only God can give. We put ourselves where God can meet our needs and, through us, the needs of others.

Jesus lived by this kind of prayer, and he taught his disciples to do the same. As he talked with them at the Last Supper, he said several times that he would give them whatever they asked for in his name (John 14:13,14; 15:16). He told them that through asking in his name, they were going to continue his ministry by doing the things he had done and even greater things (John 14:12)! Praying in the name of Jesus is not about using certain words as a magic formula to get what we want. "In my name" refers to a vital personal relationship between Jesus and the believer. This relationship is such that we want to see Jesus' purposes fulfilled in ourselves, the church, and the world around us. A phrase in the Lord's Prayer captures this desire: "Your will be done, on earth as it is in heaven" (Matt. 6:10). As we give ourselves to do what Jesus wants, he promises to provide what we need to do his will. Living in the flow of this prayerful obedience produces growth in the life of faith. Little by little, as we pray, we are changed into people who want God to be at the center of their lives.

We learn the path of prayer by praying. No amount of reading books or attending prayer groups is a substitute for opening mind and heart in talking and listening to God frequently and honestly. As we open ourselves to God, God will reveal himself to us. As we pray, we will be given eyes to see God's power at work around us. As we begin to recognize God's voice and see God's fingerprints all over our world, we will be drawn into prayers of thanksgiving. We will then offer ourselves more fully to God so that God's power flows more strongly. This dynamic will go deeper and deeper over time, and faith will become the major reality by which we live.

If we want to be more fully available to God, a prayer like the following is enough of a raised sail to begin the process: "God, I trust that your will is the best thing that can happen to me today. Let your will be done in everything, no matter what it is. Make me a graceful presence wherever I go. In, around, through, and in spite of me, let your will be done on earth as it is in heaven." Leave this desire of your heart with God as you go out to meet the day, and trust God to be faithful.

## Obedience

Sailing requires us to acknowledge that God is sovereign and to give God our obedience. In the Sailboat church there is only one Master, one Captain, and it is not us! We are the crew, and our role is to do the Master's will. It is very tempting to think otherwise. It is human nature to assume that our ideas must be the same as God's ideas. This is how most churches get to be rowboats in the first place. Everything in our culture tells us that if we are smart enough, rich enough, and talented enough, we can do anything we want. That may be true in the kingdoms of this world, but it is emphatically not true in the kingdom of God. One of the basic truths of sailing is that we don't make the wind blow.

If we are to be sailing partners with God, we must be willing to let God lead from the very beginning. This means submitting our vision of what Sailboat church would look like to God for testing and trial. Rather than grabbing the oars and starting a turn-the-church-into-a-Sailboat committee, the place to begin is to let God move to the center of our own lives and take control of us. The birthing of a Sailboat church is much more personal and relational than organizational.

*Obedience* is an unpopular word in our culture. It implies that we are losing something. Our life and our freedom are somehow diminished. And yet, the posture of obedience is at the heart of spiritual sailing. Raising the sail of obedience allows us to partner with God. Without this partnership, Sailboat church cannot happen.

One way to get a better grip on what obedience means is to look at the life of Jesus. He was absolutely obedient, surrendered, and given over to God. Every thought, action, and desire came from his passion to be in the flow of God's will. He calls us to live this same kind of life. "If any want to become my followers, let them deny themselves and take up their cross and follow me. For those who want to save their life will lose it, and those who lose their life for my sake will surely find it" (Matt. 16:24–25).

In meditating on his life, death, and resurrection, we can get beyond our culture's degraded definitions of obedience to catch a vision of our true calling in life. What God has in store for us is the best possible thing that could ever happen. Like Jesus, when we raise the sail of obedience we move through life powered by the grace and power of God.

So it must be with us if we want to be engaged in Sailboat church. When we are charting the course, God has a hard time taking us where God wants us to go. As long as we are pursuing self-generated agendas that seem good to us, God has little room to work out God's agenda among us. The bottom line is that God is meant to lead and we are meant to follow in this thing we call church. When God is in control, we will find ourselves sailing. When we insist on being in control, we will usually find ourselves rowing.

This posture of obedience is both intensely personal and deeply corporate. On the personal side, only you can give your life over to God. On the corporate side, your offering of yourself to God daily as a living sacrifice will have significant impact on those around you. These two realities work together in the birthing of a Sailboat congregation. It is impossible to lead others into sailing unless one is raising the sail of obedience in her or his own life.

## Discernment

Nothing changes the actual life of a congregation more than practicing discernment in making decisions. Discernment is the way Sailboat churches navigate their way into God's will. We may read all the available books on sailing while practicing all the moves of sailing, but unless we actually begin to let our decisions (and how we make them) be shaped by the Holy Spirit, we will never sail.

God is very willing to guide us if we are willing to be guided. This willingness requires us to slow down, have the inner intention to seek God's will, learn to be sensitive to signs of God's activity and calling in the world, and develop some facility in listening to God's voice in Scripture, circumstances, and community. Rowers who want to become sailors will intentionally change the way they make decisions to allow God to be more involved. This process is so crucial to sailing that a whole chapter of this book is devoted to it. Chapter 10 offers a basic orientation to this way of being with God. Further resources for the practice of discernment as individuals and in groups are listed at the end of the book.

## Sacrifice

If we want the Spirit of God to be the prime mover in our church, there are some things that will have to go. The biblical word for this letting go is *sacrifice*. The particular list of obstacles and idols will vary from congregation to congregation. But in most church, two things consistently block God: the need for control and the need for comfort. Adopting a posture of sacrifice, of letting go, in these two areas will go a long way in helping the church set sail.

*1. The Need for Control.* Our human need to be in control often blocks God's wishes. At the heart of this attitude is the sin that led Adam and Eve astray. Genesis tells the sad story of how the first human beings broke fellowship with God by doing what seemed good to them, contrary to God's command. They needed to be in control.

The struggle to be in control is still very much with us and in us. It is a kind of addiction that is part of our fallen human nature. Even the most passionate lovers of God must deal with layer upon layer of what writer Thomas Merton called the "false self."[1] This is the self that is always protecting those things that make us happy, safe, and comfortable. Jesus consistently turned away from this false self throughout his life in order to do God's will. At times his struggle was very painful. In the garden of Gethsemane, as Jesus faced the desire to save himself and avoid the cross, his agony produced sweat like great drops of blood (Luke 22:39–44).

When we stubbornly insist on our own way or treat others harshly in order to achieve our own ends, it is obvious that we are not centered on God. But a deeper truth is that even when we spend our time, energy, and money on the needs and wants of others, our false self is always ready to see what's in it for us. Psychologists tell stories of people who seemed to be selfless servants of others but who were actually driven by desperate needs to manipulate, please, and control. When we believe we are in control of things, we feel safe. When we face the reality that God is really in control, we are thrown into the realm of faith. We must trust in what we cannot yet see. In God's realm, if we do not stand by faith, we do not stand at all.

God cannot give our churches everything God wants us to have until we let go of our need to be in control of the church and, through faith, let God take charge. If Jesus, the Son of God, had to give up control over his life in the garden of Gethsemane, what makes us think that God is going to take us and our churches by a different path? Actually, it is a great relief to let God take God's rightful place as Lord and head of the church and take our places as junior partners in God's work. The yoke becomes easy and the burden light.

I imagine that most of what was happening with the believers, between the ascension of Jesus and Pentecost day, had to do with sacrificing control. They had to let go of what they thought the agenda was. They had to let go of the idea that they already had what it took to move into God's future. They had to feel their powerlessness before they could be open to receive the power of the Holy Spirit. They had to know in their deepest selves that they were only clay jars (2 Cor. 4:7) before God could pour God's treasure into them. So it was that as the wind of the Spirit began to blow on Pentecost, Peter stood before the gathered crowd and talked, not about himself or the other disciples, not about their plans or ideas, but instead about Jesus and about God's gracious work to save the world through him.

*2. The Need to Be Comfortable.* Another thing we must sacrifice in order to move with the Spirit is our need to be comfortable. It is human nature to seek comfort and to flee discomfort. One of the places we may seek comfort and stability in an uncomfortable, unstable world is church. Sometimes our need for comfort at church causes us to resist change or anything else that makes us uncomfortable. This can present great challenges for church leaders: they may spend great amounts of time and energy making sure that people in the congregation are comfortable. Keeping them comfortable prevents complaints and other actions that make others uncomfortable. But an addiction to comfort in the church tends to lead toward more rowing than sailing.

Jesus seemed to make people uncomfortable on a regular basis. He called his first disciples into an enterprise that turned their lives upside down, making them and their families very uncomfortable. He said things that often made the crowds listening to him uncomfortable, such as, "Go sell all that you have, give it to the poor, then come and follow me" (see Matt. 19:21); "Give to everyone who asks of you and do not refuse those who would borrow from you" (see 5:42); and "love your enemies" (v. 44). To be a follower of Jesus is, by definition, to follow a path that will take us out of our range of comfort on a regular basis.

One congregation experienced this need to let go of being comfortable when they invited a Spanish-speaking immigrant fellowship to

worship on Sunday afternoons in their church building. The governing board of the congregation felt that it was God's will and a good
thing for the two groups to share an under-used building. The two
groups slowly grew to know each other and enjoy their relationship.

However, in time, the cultural and language differences and the
different needs of the two ministries began to create friction. While
still agreeing that the relationship was a good thing, the board members grew weary of the problems that kept popping up. At one meeting an astute member said, "We do have quite a few issues to work
out with our Spanish-speaking friends, but these kinds of relationships are always going to involve some give and take on all sides.
Part of our problem is that we are expecting things to be just like
they were when we were in these buildings by ourselves. That's not
a reasonable expectation! These problems do make us uncomfortable. They do require extra effort on the part of everyone. But isn't
that a small price to pay for all the blessings we receive from this
relationship?"

This leader was challenging fellow believers to let go of being as
comfortable as they once were in order to be Sailboat Christians. In
response, they once again committed wholeheartedly to doing what
it would take to make the relationship with the Spanish-speaking fellowship work. Generally speaking, human nature is averse to this
kind of sacrifice. It will happen only as the Holy Spirit enables us to
let go of our need to be comfortable.

## Trust God's Provision

The Bible speaks of faith as "the assurance of things hoped for, the
conviction of things not seen" (Heb. 11:1). This kind of faith in God
and God's promises is another essential sail to be raised in the Sailboat church. It makes a crucial difference in how we live together in
the church.

Let's observe, for example, the governing board of Corinth Church
as it meets in December to work on the next year's budget. First, the
treasurer makes the financial report and gives the board a figure for
expected income for the coming year. She projects that giving will
be down because some members have died and others are moving

out of town. Second, the board spends the next three hours trying to figure out how to keep all the current programs going and also pay the bills for staff and utilities on less income than last year. The tone of the meeting becomes bleak as the evening drags on. Tempers are strained as frustrated leaders compete for their committee's share of the shrinking dollar pool. Finally, many leave the meeting depressed and wondering why they ever thought serving on the board of their church was a good idea.

These people are engaging in what might be called money-in-the-bank thinking. This is the way rowboat churches think about resources for ministry. Money-in-the-bank thinking bases the design for the future life and mission of the church almost entirely on the present reality. The determining factor in planning is what can be reasonably expected next year based on this year.

For many churches, this kind of thinking governs not only finances but also every area of the church's life. They look at the facilities they currently have and design a mission that can be carried out in those facilities. Counting volunteers in the church dictates what mission or programs they can handle without too much stress. The possibilities before the congregation are whittled down to what is manageable given the resources at hand. This way of functioning keeps the church well within its comfort zone. Potential for failure and the need for risk or sacrifice are minimized. The result, however, is that vision for the future is shaped primarily by what they lack. This is rowing at it finest.

If the early Christians had operated like this, the church never would have gotten out of Jerusalem. Their list of assets was pitifully short. The early church had no budget, no buildings, and no paid staff. They did have, however, a passionate commitment to Jesus Christ and the belief that with God all things are possible.

We see them accessing these spiritual assets shortly after Pentecost as Peter and John encounter a crippled beggar. It was the custom in that day for people going to or from worship to give alms to beggars. As the disciples approached, the man asked them for money, expecting the normal handout. "But Peter said, 'I have no silver or gold, but what I have I give you; in the name of Jesus Christ of Nazareth, stand up and walk' . . . and immediately his feet and ankles were made strong" (Acts 3:6–7). Peter's lack of funds did not keep him from ministering to this man. By faith in the risen Christ, he had access to resources far beyond the limitations of his empty pocketbook.

Sailboat churches know that money and resources are never the most important issue when it comes to the mission of the church. When a church is busy doing what God wants it to do, the resources will be provided. Exciting things happen in the church when leaders move away from a money-in-the-bank mentality and start focusing instead on seeking and doing God's will in everything.

The Christian life was never meant to be something that we do ourselves. God desires to have a deep and intimate partnership with us in blessing the whole world. The deeper we allow God to go with us, the more we will experience God's guidance and provision in every area of our lives. Prayer is the means by which this process goes forward. Prayer opens the door for God's grace and provision to flow into our lives, into the church, and into the world.

In contrast to Corinth Church, when the board of Christ Church met in May for its annual planning retreat, the board members spent some time reviewing the church's mission statement and the long- and short-term goals of their church. They evaluated how things were going in the church in light of those goals. In a time of worship and thanksgiving, they celebrated the past year's achievements such as sending a short-term mission team to Honduras and becoming a founding participant in their town's first food pantry for needy families.

After worship, they took time both individually and as a group to meditate on, pray over, and discuss together the question "What is God calling our church to be and do in the coming year?" Based on what came out of this discussion and prayer, they considered a number of possible new ministries for the coming year. When this work was completed, the officers took home a list of all the possibilities, promising to pray about them until the next meeting.

When they met a month later, again the key question before them was, "What is God calling us to be and do in the coming year?" They began with an hour of prayer and reflection on Scripture. Then they shared and discussed the fruit of their individual meditations on the list of possible ministries from the last meeting. During this discussion, some items were deleted from the list by common consent; one new possibility was added. Again, after a time of reflection and prayer for God's will to be done, these leaders were asked to pray for guidance until the next meeting. The pastor announced that he would be in the sanctuary in prayer on these matters each Tuesday morning at 7:00 a.m. and invited the board members to join him.

At the next meeting, board members were asked to mark their top three choices on the list of possible new or expanded ministries. Five ministries rose naturally to the top of the list. Passionate discussion ensued regarding the choices and which were most appropriate for the next year. After listening to one another and taking several more votes, two of the possibilities emerged as ministries the great majority of board members felt the church was being led to do in the next year. Next came the hardest question: were there any missions or ministries the leaders felt God was leading the church to stop doing? After discussing this question the meeting closed in worship, and the group pledged to pray together about these things in the weeks ahead.

The process continued bathed in prayer until in November the board met to plan the budget for the New Year. The meeting began with worship and prayer for guidance. The session was asked to think once again on the question, "What is it that God wants us to do this coming year?" The treasurer then made the financial report. Projected giving was down due to some members moving away.

The leaders had difficult decisions to make about money and mission. Through it all, however, they had the sense that God was guiding them and that God would provide what was needed to accomplish what they were supposed to do. Instead of competing to get their piece of the shrinking pie, the board members worked together to figure out how to carry the work forward. At the end of the meeting, they adjourned to the sanctuary where they dedicated the mission plan and budget for the coming year to God.

Many left the sanctuary feeling excited about what God might do and glad to have been a part of it all. They had raised the sail of faith in God's provision and guidance for the church's mission. The planning process was based on the belief (or at least a strong suspicion) that God "by the power at work within us is able to accomplish abundantly far more than all we can ask or imagine" (Eph. 3:20). For these board members, church was an adventure in sailing under the power of the Spirit.

## Expectant Gathering

Along with prayer, one of the most central spiritual practices of the early church was gathering, getting together with fellow believers. The picture we see in the first chapter of Acts is of a gathered group waiting for something to happen. Jesus had instructed them to go back to Jerusalem and "wait for the promise of the Father" (Acts 1:4). On Pentecost day, "they were all together in one place" (2:1). Again, the story repeats that on Pentecost "All who believed were together . . ." (v. 44). All this and much more in Acts points to how important being together was to the first Christians. From its earliest days, Christianity was a communal faith.

In carrying on the practice of gathering, the disciples and other early believers were faithful to their Jewish roots. Yet the immediate post-Pentecost church had reasons for gathering other than Jewish custom. They believed that Jesus' promise was true: "Where two or three are gathered in my name, I am there among them" (Matt. 18:20). They met because, indeed, Jesus had not left them orphaned but came to them in the power of the Spirit, especially when they were together. So they got together regularly to worship, to pray for all kinds of needs, to eat, to discern, and to commission persons for service. They gathered because they expected Jesus to show up.

Those who want to grow in the life of the Spirit today will al￭ want to practice expectant gathering. Whenever believers mee￭ the church or beyond its walls, we can expect the Spirit of Je￭ meet us and to work in us and through us. Small groups ￭ for study, prayer, mission, or mutual support can all expe￭ power of God moving among them as they gather ex￭ faith and prayer.

While these opportunities are good, the weekly ￭ community for worship in word and sacrament i￭ opportunity for expectant gathering. How sad it ￭ have forgotten to expect anything from going beyond some social interaction and a little ship, sacraments, and the proclamation of t￭ to change us! God invites us into the fell￭ munity to be transformed and empowe￭ to encounter us in our worship, and are ￭

offering ourselves in worship as living sacrifices? This is what worship is really all about.

The way pastors, musicians, and others participate in worship makes a difference in what people expect when they come to worship. Leaders who are engaged with God on an intimate level convey this possibility to the congregation in the way they lead services. The tone of the music, the sermon, the Scripture readings, and the prayers carry a message about how near God is and what to expect of God. Even the expressions on the faces of worship leaders and choir members influence the tone of the service. When people look at those leading worship, do they see people who are themselves worshiping God? Do they sense that the leaders of worship are expecting and experiencing God's presence? Is there something about how worship is led that points beyond the leader to God?

The apostle Paul talked about the subtle chemistry between the gospel and those who bear it to others, "We have this treasure in clay jars" (2 Cor. 4:7). We are not the treasure. However, in the way we approach participation in worship we can either discount and obscure the treasure or we can point to it and invite others to experience it. Perhaps the best prayer that worship leaders of all kinds can pray is, "God, I know I am a clay jar. But you have also called me to lead in worship. So let there be a treasure in this clay jar today, let your people be blessed, and may all the glory go to you."

Beyond the tone of worship, expectant prayer occurring during and around the worship service is a powerful way to cooperate with the Holy Spirit. Make it a habit to pray for the coming Sunday gatherings for education and worship every time believers meet. People can also intentionally pray for the service as it goes on. In one congregation, this ministry was taken on by the church officers. Each Sunday, one of them was stationed in a room near the sanctuary to pray for the congregation and worship leaders during the service.

God loves to respond to the needs of God's people. To help people experience this truth, opportunities for more intense prayer can also be offered after the service. A congregation with which I am familiar has Stephen ministers stationed in the chapel each Sunday after worship. Persons who need someone to pray with or for them are urged to go there. Those who wait to pray with such seekers should be expecting God's graceful presence and hopeful for those who come. In this intimate context of expectant gathering, the power of the Spirit can be experienced in profound ways.

## Thanksgiving and Testimony

When the wind of the Spirit begins to blow and the church begins to sail, it is important to give God the glory. The fact that exciting things are happening points us to the reality and possibility of God's power among us. Seeing God's Spirit at work moves us to a place of deep thanksgiving. Thanksgiving reminds us that what we are experiencing is God at work, not simply the result of our smart planning and hard work.

One form thanksgiving can take is that of testimony, verbal or written reports of how God has acted in someone's life, within the church, or in the world outside the church. The practice of testimony goes all the way back to the Psalms, as believers recounted the mighty works of God and called on one another to give God praise. Testimony encourages believers. It also witnesses to seekers about God's presence, care, and power. It can be practiced in the worship service and encouraged in small group meetings.

True testimony always focuses more on God than on the one speaking. The point is not how bad, sick, confused, straying, or immoral the believer was, but rather how wonderful and powerful God is. Neither do testimonies have to be dramatic to be effective. One of the best I ever heard came from a woman who taught the second grade Sunday school class. She talked simply and lovingly about how she had experienced God's presence in the midst of her class and how it had changed her. Jesus told us not to hide our lights under a bushel basket, but rather to let them shine so that all might see. Testimony is one of the ways we do this to the glory of God.

❊ ❊ ❊ ❊ ❊ ❊ ❊

The wind of the Spirit is blowing today just as much as when the first believers sailed out to make disciples of all nations. God has everything we need to be faithful in our mission and discipleship and is more than willing to give it to us as we humbly allow ourselves to be guided by the Holy Spirit. Raise the sails and cast off!

## Questions for Reflection

1. Draw a circle representing your life. Make a mark in the circle representing how close God is to the center of your life. How does this relationship with God empower your life and ministry as a Christian?
2. How much quality time do you generally spend paying attention to God each day? Each week?
3. How do you see money-in-the-bank thinking at work in your church? When have you seen the church move beyond it in faith?
4. When was a time that you had to move outside your comfort zone to be faithful to God?

Chapter 8

# Moving with the Wind

*R*owing involves sitting in a boat and pulling on the oars to move forward. Sailing involves raising the sails and then moving them to catch the wind. Sailors know that how they move with the wind is important. Certain kinds of movements will send the boat in one direction, and other movements will send it elsewhere. Similarly, in the Sailboat church, how we live in response to the presence of the Holy Spirit is important. Some actions generate positive energy with the Spirit while others blunt the Spirit's power among us. This chapter will look at practices that give the Spirit more freedom to fill the church's sails.

## Be Intentional about Spiritual Formation

The early churches practiced a communal life that allowed the Holy Spirit to fill and use them. The key word here is *communal*. Many Christians engage in a variety of spiritual disciplines and practices individually. This is usually a very good thing. People who come to church brimming over with God-life have something to share that gives energy to the whole body. However, the disciplines of individuals are not what have the most impact on the life of a church.

Rather it is the disciplines engaged in as a congregation that are most powerful. These practices allow the Spirit to move each church into the adventure that God has for it. It would not be appropriate to write a one-size-fits-all prescription of spiritual practices for every church because the most helpful ones will vary from congregation to congregation depending on its situation and mission. Instead, here is a list of questions to think through prayerfully together. As you discern areas that need attention, begin to take them before God, asking God to lead you to resources and ideas that are right for your church.

- How in our life together do we make time for people to experience God in ways that empower them?
- How do we challenge and support people to move out of their comfort zones to serve God?
- How deeply is prayer woven into the fabric of our communal life? How can we make the practice of prayer more central?
- How does our congregational culture encourage generosity, including tithing, as a spiritual discipline?
- What is the passion level of our worship? Does our worship encourage people to offer themselves to God every week? Does our worship provide opportunities for people to experience what is being preached and taught?
- Is testimony from members of the congregation a regular part of our worship?
- Where in our congregation do people get beyond surface relationships to share their struggles and know one another deeply?
- What signs do we see of maturing fruit of the Spirit in our people? Where do we need more?
- How do we as a congregation practice genuine hospitality to strangers and "the least of these"?
- How do we confront behaviors that are hurtful to the body of Christ? How do we help people change these behaviors?
- What opportunities do we offer for people not only to learn the Scriptures but also to be transformed by them?
- What things do we as a congregation need to stop doing so that we can focus more energy in growing toward God and doing God's mission in the world?
- How could our board, working with the minister, become a more effective spiritual leadership team?
- How do we hold our leaders accountable and support them in their spiritual growth?
- Where in our congregation do we practice Jesus' command to "love one another as I have loved you" (John 15:12)?

- How do we encourage people to share with people outside the congregation how God has made a difference in their lives?

Asking the right questions is powerful. Reflecting on these questions can help a church shape its life so that it can move nimbly with the Spirit.

## Practice Sanctified Imagination

There are hundreds of good things we could be doing at any given time, numberless needs in the world that could be addressed in God's name. But not all of those are necessarily our personal responsibility as individuals or congregations. God means for us to take on some needs while other needs constitute a calling for other churches. Each congregation must discover its own mission; each one must discern what is beside its name on God's to-do list.

Sailboat congregations use their Holy Spirit-led imagination to see beyond what is to what could be. They take the general principles of the faith, hold those up against the context in which they live, and ask: "What will it look like for us to be faithful to God's call at this particular place and time?" They make the mental leap from abstract biblical principles to concrete ways to act. They imagine their way from learning the principle to living the principle. As they let the Holy Spirit work in their imaginations, God uses them to bring this world a little closer to what God wants it to be.

For instance, in the mid-1980s, Clifton Church in Atlanta felt a call to help the increasing number of homeless people on the streets. After much prayer and discussion, it decided to begin a night shelter at the church. The surprising thing about this decision was that the congregation at that time had about thirty members and was meeting in a smallish house that had been remodeled into a church building. The church had no special funding, few volunteers, and limited facilities. Yet each evening, members of the church began going to the inner city in their own cars and transporting homeless men back to the church. There the men were given a warm welcome, a hot meal, and a safe place to sleep on the floor of the sanctuary. So began the first night shelter for homeless people in the city of Atlanta, Georgia. This particular mission came into being because the members of the church were able to imagine what faithfulness to God might look like in their own particular setting.

It could reasonably be argued that the malaise in many churches today is due, at least in part, to a failure of imagination. When we cannot imagine God doing a new thing among us, the energy and excitement go out of church life. We tend to spend our time continuing the past or holding on to the present. It is not enough to believe only in theory that God is able to do new and exciting things in our midst. God calls us to be active partners in the adventure. Christians who want to sail with the Spirit will always be asking God what the repentant crowds asked John the Baptist: "What then should we do?" (Luke 3:10). In answer, God enables the faithful to dream dreams and see visions.

By advocating the use of sanctified imagination, I'm not implying that Christians are justified in acting like loose cannons, rampaging through the church doing whatever comes into their minds. The appropriate use of this spiritual gift of imagination is rooted first in a deep sense of what it entails to be Jesus' disciples and second in a clear understanding of what Christian faithfulness means and has meant in times past. A firm grounding in Scripture is also essential, not so that we can quote reams of biblical text from memory, but rather so that we are steeped in the full witness of Scripture to the point that it shapes how we think, act, and make decisions. Instead of using Scripture to further our ends, we must have the humility to let Scripture judge and transform us.

## Rise above Self-Interest for the Good of the Church

Parents will tell you that raising children often involves sacrificing your desires for their sake. You get up for the 2:00 a.m. feeding when you would much rather stay in bed. You would love to sit down with the paper when you get home from work, but instead you take your child to soccer practice. You may prefer a pricey new car, but you buy the cheaper used model and put the difference into the savings account for college. Parents are called to rise above their own self-interests and preferences when necessary in the interest of their children. Sailboat Christians may also be called to give up what we want for the good of others and to further the mission of God's church.

For instance, personal preferences regarding the worship service have torn churches apart. In negotiating what has been called "the worship wars,"[1] it is important to understand that much of the furor is about style rather than substance. The controversy often turns on one group's preference for a formal or more traditional service with organ music and songs sung out of a hymnal and another's for something less traditional, perhaps a more free-flowing service with contemporary songs led by a praise team or band.

Unfortunately, battle lines are sometimes drawn around these preferences. Those who want a more informal style of worship may feel hurt and angry when others react negatively to their requests for change. The choir director, choir, or organist may feel threatened when asked to lead, sing, or play music they don't like. Those who prefer contemporary music may complain that they aren't being spiritually fed by hymns from the hymnal. The preacher may be afraid of being asked to preach a more informal sermon without a pulpit or notes. None of these reactions have to do with the essence of worship itself: that the gospel is truly preached and God is rightly glorified. They grow out of the natural human desire to have things the way we like them, especially at church.

In Sailboat congregations, people work together to discern what style of worship and configuration of worship services best furthers the mission of the church. To do this, they must rise above their own personal desires and preferences for worship. The worship committee of Main Street Church came to realize that its location was becoming a mission field. Their church was located near a growing university and more students were moving in around the church building. They'd tried repeatedly to attract the students to their traditional 11:00 a.m. service, but their efforts bore little fruit. Then, one night, a seminary intern suggested starting a Tuesday night service with music provided by a band. He invited members of the session to attend such a service at another church, and a few weeks later about half the session boarded the church van to see what this new kind of service was all about.

At the next committee meeting, discussion was lively. "I could hardly wait to get out of there," said one person. "The music gave me a headache." Another member noted that the room had been overflowing with college students and that they seemed to respond enthusiastically to the pastor's sermon. As the discussion turned to the possibility of having a similar service at their church, one of the older members spoke: "I hate that kind of music, and I would probably never come to this new service. But if doing this might help us reach young people that we might not otherwise reach for Christ, I am all for it." His comment helped focus the committee's attention on what was most important, the mission of the church instead of personal preferences about music.

This way of moving with the wind involves humility of spirit. It requires that we realize that because something is right for us does not mean it is right for everyone; because we prefer doing things a certain way does not mean that is always the best way to do them. It involves the ability to stand back and look at the big picture when making decisions instead of always doing what we would prefer. Sometimes it may mean sacrificing our own personal desires and interests so that the mission of the church may go forward. Sailboat Christians are willing to rise above self-interest and personal preference for the greater good of the whole. In so doing, they follow the example of Jesus who came, not to be served, but to serve.

## The Willingness to Risk and Fail

The Gospel of Matthew tells the parable of the Talents in chapter 25. It is about a man who entrusts to three of his servants large amounts of money (a talent was worth about fifteen years of wages for a laborer). Then the man goes away on a long journey. When he returns, he calls the servants for an accounting. Two of the servants have used the money left in their charge to make a profit for the master. They are praised and rewarded. The third servant, however, motivated by fear, has buried the master's money in the ground for safekeeping. He comes before the master, bringing back the money he had been given, expecting no doubt to receive a commendation for returning the talent safe and sound. Instead, he gets a scathing rebuke and is thrown "into the outer darkness where there will be weeping and gnashing of teeth" (v. 30).

What did this third servant do wrong? The story seems to say that his sin was in conserving the talent. He was judged harshly, not for losing the talent, but for failing to try to do anything with it. He felt that his primary job was to save what the master had entrusted to him. His nightmare was losing it. Fear of failure kept him from taking a risk with what he had been given, and for this he was thrown into the outer darkness.

It is important for Sailboat Christians to be clear about their call. What are we to be doing in God's name, and what does it mean to be successful? Our culture holds out a particular image of success: it's big and profitable; it involves positive numbers and positive cash flow. To succeed is to be a star, a hit, a winner. Success is victory, triumph, and achievement. Failure is the absence of these things.

If we look to the life of Jesus for a definition of success, however, we see a different picture. By the world's measure, he never achieved success in his work and died a failure at a relatively young age. Jesus had every opportunity and all the gifts necessary to succeed according to the world's definition. But he chose another way. Jesus never saw his mission through the lens of worldly success. He knew his call was to be faithful to God and to God's will. In a strange way, Jesus succeeded by failing. This is the mystery of the cross. In his obedient death, a great failure and scandal in the eyes of his contemporaries, he reached ultimate success in faithfulness to God.

Many churches wither and die because they are afraid of trying and failing. Like the third servant in the parable, they are afraid to take the risks necessary to do the Master's will. God is always going ahead of us, doing new things and inviting us to join in. Trying something new usually involves the possibility that it may not work. Investing in new ministries may call for a significant outlay of money without any guarantee of return. Those who crave success cannot abide the possibility of failure. So rather than risk losing what God has given to the church, they turn into guardians of a building, a balanced budget, a tradition, or an endowment. Rather than being in mission, their main responsibility becomes protecting and conserving the church's assets.

Sailboat congregations live out the truth that success is about faithfulness, which sometimes requires taking risks. They know that God calls us to walk by faith and not by sight, and they are willing to call one another to take a leap of faith when it seems necessary to do God's will. They are willing to risk what God has given for the sake of doing God's will. The risks may involve the church's finances, the church's buildings, or even the church's reputation in the community. This can be a frightening call. But those who are willing in faith to take the risk will receive the commendation of the Master: "Well done, good and faithful servant" (Matt. 25:23 NIV).

## Cultivate a Culture of Abundance and Generosity

Many congregations have a culture of scarcity. They believe that the resources available to them are limited. They worry about money. Many members, no matter how well off they may be, fret about personal finances and fear they will not have enough. At the root of this anxiety is the functional atheism discussed in chapter 2. If God is distant and uninvolved in our lives, holding tightly to what we have is a natural response. This dynamic helps explain why the overall percentage of giving among mainline American Christians is between 2 and 3 percent of income.

Sailboat congregations are intentional about working toward a culture of spiritual abundance and generosity based on God's faithfulness. As the Holy Spirit begins to work in the church, this work becomes easier. Experiencing God's presence and activity helps people to trust God's provision. People who trust God to provide are more willing to give. It is the abundance and faithfulness of God that evokes generous giving.

Since ancient times, the minimum of faithful giving has been the tithe. This practice of giving 10 percent of income is a countercultural leap of faith. It pushes us into a place of radical trust in God. It makes us put our money where our faith is in ways that can transform us.

Unfortunately, many people assume that tithing is beyond them. The challenge to take this leap of faith should not be held over the heads of people like a club. Guilt will not produce true generosity. Only the Holy Spirit can change tight fists into open hands. However,

Sailboat Christians will take the tithe seriously as a standard for giving. As this practice begins to make a difference in people's lives, the idea of growing toward tithing can become part of the church's teaching, preaching, and prayer. Over time, a culture of scarcity can become a culture of generosity, giving God much with which to work.

## Discern and Use the Spiritual Gifts of Members

In his letter to the Corinthians, the apostle Paul explains to the Corinthian church that God gives spiritual gifts to the members of the church to empower the church for its mission (1 Cor. 12:4–11). In today's church, unfortunately, the expectation often seems to be that all the spiritual gifts the congregation needs will be concentrated in the pastor. This is not a biblical idea, and when it is put into practice it can do serious damage to a church's health.

Sailboat churches know that every single person in the congregation has gifts for ministry. When a high proportion of members actively put their gifts to work toward God's mission for that church, the church will sail farther and faster. When, in contrast, all the gifts must come from the pastor, or perhaps the pastor and a few leaders, the church will suffer. For this reason, Sailboat congregations make it a priority to help people find their spiritual gifts and put their gifts to work for God's sake.

Instead of helping members find their ministries, rowboat churches settle for recruiting warm bodies to hold positions. "How many slots do we have to fill?" is often the guiding question for nominating and other committees. They draft people to do things for which those individuals have no gifts or inclination, just to meet institutional quotas. This kind of attitude sets people up to fail. It certainly denies them the joy of discovering and using the special gifts God gave them for ministry.

Many Christians can tell stories of volunteering to do something absolutely foreign to their gifts and experience, finding that the Spirit equipped them as they went along. The more biblical pattern, however, seems to be that God places people and gifts in the church to carry forward the kinds of mission God wants to happen there. For example, a church with many people who love to teach could start an after-school program or a Bible-study ministry in the local jail. A church with seasoned people of prayer might consider a ministry of intercession and healing. A church with many folks who have the gift of hospitality could sponsor refugee families. The possibilities are endless; the point is helping people find and use the gifts that God has given them.

Exciting things can happen if, instead of slotting people into jobs to keep on doing what your church has always done before, its mission is shaped at least partly by the gifts God has given its members. It may feel risky at first to do this; some positions might not get filled. You may also discover new energy bubbling up in your congregation as people experience the joy of employing their God-given gifts.

Joyfulness happens partly because serving in ministry and mission can be a major avenue of spiritual growth. Such service can intensify a person's dependence on God and open up deeper avenues of prayer and commitment. The shift from doing institutional maintenance to being in ministry for God also tends to attract new people into the active core of the church. People who would never agree to serve on a committee can do something active to forward the ministry of their church. Even homebound people can have a ministry of prayer or give pastoral care over the telephone or by email. Ministries and gifts are varied, but the one Spirit is in all of them and will touch the lives of those who try to use their gifts in God's service.

It has been pointed out that in many churches 20 percent of the people do 80 percent of the work. Often that 20 percent is overburdened and weary, and the 80 percent tend to be passive consumers of the programs and ministries provided by the pastor and the 20 percent. This is rowboat behavior. Sailboat congregations work toward the goal of having all members involved in ministry that both feeds and challenges them to the end that the mission of the church will go forward and God will be glorified. This is how people find joy in serving God!

## Love One Another

From the beginning, the Christian community was to be marked by a special kind of relationship. Jesus talks about this relationship in his last address to this disciples: "This is my commandment, that you love one another as I have loved you. No one has greater love than this, to lay down one's life for one's friends" (John 15:12–13). On that same night, he began to show them what this kind of love looks like when he abandoned the place of honor at the dinner table and stooped to wash his disciples' feet. After doing this work usually done by servants, Jesus said, "I have set you an example, that you also should do as I have done to you" (13:15).

What passes for love in our culture is basically a positive response to what is pleasing, attractive, and easy to love. This love is natural to self-centered human beings. Jesus' command to love one another as he loved us in humble service pushes us beyond natural human love into the realm of supernatural love, the kind of love shown by Jesus on the cross. The essence of this love is seen as Jesus forgives those who are crucifying him. Sailboat churches have the courage to move beyond surface social interactions and call people to interact at deeper levels of intimacy. Moving into this way of relating brings us face to face with all the rough edges that hide under the surface of people being nice to one another in a normal social setting.

The command to love this way engages us in a supernatural enterprise. It pushes us beyond what we can do in our human power and makes us call on God to create this Jesus-shaped love in us and through us. It is an "in-spite-of" love that calls us to accept people as they really are and also to be known intimately by others. Churches develop these relationships only by the power of the Holy Spirit. As they do push deeper into exploring what it means to love one another as Christ has loved them, the church's life becomes an experience of the reign of God on earth to those inside the church and a vibrant witness to those outside the church.

## Grow through Hard Times

Since even the most faithful Christians cannot avoid times of trial and trouble, we may as well make the most of them! We can do this by using what life throws at us to grow deeper in the faith. Part of this growth comes from understanding how God is present and working in these painful situations. Three biblical principles are especially important in giving us a spiritual understanding of difficult situations: (1) God can bring good out of anything; (2) God can use our weaknesses; and (3) God leads, and we follow.

*God Can Bring Good Out of Anything.* Romans 8:28 states: "We know that all things work together for good for those who love God, who are called according to his purpose." Christians have used this verse since the early days of the faith to find comfort and hope when things go wrong. The central thrust of the passage is one of redemption. There is no situation from which the grace of God is excluded. God is always at work to mine good out of our failure and disappointments. Another way to say this is that God never wastes anything. God can use even our sins, mistakes, and tragedies to further God's purposes for us and for God's kingdom.

Living into the truth that God can work in all things for good helps believers maintain a healthy and humble hope. This hope is not based on how skilled, competent, or holy we are. Rather it takes into account that we are all human beings who fail regularly in spite of our best intentions, and in addition to dealing with our own failures and sins, we must also deal with the sins and mistakes of others. To say that God works for good in all things is to say that nothing can keep God's will from being done in and among us. God is stronger than anything that can come at us. To believe in God's sovereignty is to put no boundaries on God's ability to use whatever life sends our way to further God's purposes. It is to trust that in the end, God's will shall be done on earth as in heaven.

The most bitter disappointment and the sharpest grief can actually open the door for God to do great things. Scripture shows us that God does God's best work under the most dire circumstances and at times when everything seems lost. Recall the prophet Elijah, who stands looking at a valley full of human bones, "and they were very dry" (Ezek. 37:2). God says to him that "these bones are the whole house of Israel. They say, 'Our bones are dried up, and our hope is lost completely'" (v. 11). The Spirit of God blew across the dead dry bones, and they "stood on their feet, a vast multitude" (v. 10). Other examples include the many barren, hopeless women in Scripture who gave birth through God's intervention, and whose children grew up to do important things for God (Gen. 18:1–15; 21:1–7; 1 Sam. 1:1–28; Luke 1:1–25). The potential disaster of a hungry crowd in a deserted place with no food opened the door for Jesus to do one of his great miracles, the feeding of the five thousand (see Matt. 14:13–21). And when all seemed lost and the stone was rolled across the door of Jesus' grave, God had the last word over evil in raising him from the dead. The Bible is full of stories like these that show that, when God is involved, there are no hopeless situations.

Christians who understand this principle treat trials and road-blocks as paths to God's future instead of dead ends. One Christmas eve in the 1950s, Hemphill Church faced just such a potential dead end when its sanctuary burned to the ground. The fire was so traumatic that even decades later, when I became their pastor, members still talked about it. This beloved classic country church building had held many years of memories for the congregation and the community. The situation was even more discouraging because the church's membership had been shrinking for years. Some folks thought the fire would be the end of the church. Yet this congregation was blessed with visionary leaders who were able to look beyond the disaster of the moment to see the possibilities of a new future. The decision was made to build a new sanctuary of contemporary design where the old one had stood, and as these plans went forward, the church started to revive. Its new life and energy attracted others, and for the first time in years, the church grew. God brought new life out of the ashes.

*God Can Use Our Weaknesses.* When we think of offering ourselves to God, most of us think of offering God our strengths. We hardly ever think of offering God our weaknesses and our lacks. But remember the apostle Paul, who had what he called a thorn in the flesh, some kind of weakness or problem that he believed was hampering him in doing God's work. Three times he prayed for this thing to be taken away from him. God's answer was "My grace is sufficient for you, for [my] power is made perfect in weakness" (2 Cor. 12:9).

God can use our weaknesses as well as our strengths. In fact, sometimes our weaknesses can glorify God more than our strengths. Look at it this way: when we operate out of our strengths, the focus is on us. We are in control, and it's easy to slip into thinking that we are doing it all ourselves. We're not leaving room for God to do much. But when we operate out of our weakness, we leave God plenty of room to work. We are much more aware of God's power enabling us to do what we could never do by ourselves. The focus is on God much more than on us.

Personal weaknesses can come into sharp focus when we are called on to deal with difficult people. Jesus commanded us to "love one another as I have loved you" (John 15:12), but you may find yourself dealing with people you have a hard time tolerating, let alone loving. It is easy to avoid confessing your weakness by deciding and acting on the idea that some people are just completely unlovable. Yet the word Jesus uses to tell us to love one another is the Greek word *agape*. Agape is not romantic love; it basically means loving what is not in itself lovely or attractive. And so, Jesus is telling us to love those who are unlovely just as God loved us when we ourselves were lost in sin. We know that we will be able to deal in a positive way with difficult people only if God enables us to do it. So when we pray that God will help us to be graceful toward them, we are offering God our weakness and asking that God's power may be made perfect through our thorn in the flesh.

We are similarly encouraged to put our weaknesses in God's hands when we are asked to do something outside our comfort zones. Maybe your gifts lie in the area of property management, but your church is desperately in need of people to staff the nursery. Or you're called on to lead a committee when you've never led one before in your life. Or you're almost paralyzed with fear saying anything in front of your small Sunday school class, and now you are called on to speak in front of the congregation. Given your weaknesses, these things may seem like invitations to embarrassment and failure. Yet the God whose power is made perfect in our weakness can redeem such situations. God can give us what we need to get the job done, and God will use these experiences of weakness to teach us deeper truths. We may be humbled; we may be reminded that we are not perfect in painful ways. Yet these are opportunities for spiritual growth as we put ourselves in God's hands and let God do what God wants to do. If we always live only out of our strengths, we will never know the fullness of Christ's power dwelling in us.

When Jesus took the five loaves and two fish into his hands, he did not think about what a pittance it was to feed such a great crowd. Instead he focused on the power of God, and look what happened: he blessed and broke the bread and the story says that it was enough.

Believers who grow through trials are able to see weakness and lack as an invitation for God to do great things in them, in their churches, and in the world.

*God Leads, and We Follow.* My husband and I took dancing lessons once. I wanted to learn all those marvelous dances that you see in the old movies. My dreams hit a major snag, however, when both of us kept trying to lead. We stepped all over each other's feet, and the dancing lessons never got us anywhere. Leading and following are just as important in things spiritual as they are in dancing. God is to do the leading, and we are to do the following. Often, however, we do the leading and expect God to follow us. During the Civil War, someone asked Abraham Lincoln if he thought God was on the side of the Union. Lincoln replied that he hoped the Union was on the side of God. In the church, we often decide what to do on our own and then pray that God will be on our side and bless it. We are leading and expecting God to follow.

Sometimes it takes a failure to make us realize that we have gotten the cart before the horse. A minister I know was asked to lead a Lenten retreat at a friend's church. He accepted the invitation eagerly and confidently. He chose some of his best sermons and most inspiring talks. In due time, he packed his bags and went to take the gospel to this other congregation. About halfway through his first sermon, he realized that he was not getting through. The congregation seemed listless and half-asleep. And so it went for the rest of the weekend. No matter how lively and engaging he tried to be, nothing seemed to click with these people. He left embarrassed, feeling like a failure. It was not until some time later that he realized he had not prayed about the weekend at all. He had accepted the invitation, chosen the topics, planned the messages, and gone about the weekend confidently expecting God to follow along behind. The problem was that he hadn't invited the Holy Spirit, who could have caused the sparks of the gospel to catch fire among the people, to partner with him in leading the weekend. The temptation to take the reins out of God's hands and put them into our own is very strong and seems to be part of human nature. Failures can become blessings if they teach us that in everything that goes on in the church and in our individual ministries, God leads, and we are to follow.

## Questions for Reflection

1. Think of a time when your congregation took a significant risk. How did the members, leaders, and pastor work together to make it happen?
2. How do you react to the idea of tithing as the standard for obedient giving?
3. Does your congregation tend to have a culture of generosity or one of scarcity? What is the impact of that approach on the lives of the members?
4. How does your congregation discover people's gifts and talents and put them to work for God's mission?
5. Think about a time when you sacrificed your own desires for a great purpose. When have you seen this happen in the church?

Chapter 9

# Preparing for Storms

*B*eing a Sailboat church does not mean freedom from conflict and problems. Sometimes people have the idea that if they are fully surrendered to God and humbly trying to do God's will, the sailing will always be smooth. Not so! While storms may be unpleasant, even terrifying at times, they are a natural part of our Sailboat-church experience. In fact, it is common to encounter obstacles and conflicts just when the Spirit is moving most strongly in the church. While we may have little control over the storms of life, we can prepare for them well before they hit. The goal is to react to problems and conflicts in healthy ways and come through them stronger and wiser. Four important areas where groundwork can be done are strengthening the church's practice of prayer, developing a strong leadership team, preparing for conflict, and cultivating emotional health.

## Strengthening the Church's Practice of Prayer

Prayer is key to every aspect of being a Sailboat church, and it is especially crucial when obstacles, conflicts, and troubles arise. The depth of a congregation's relationship with God and practice of prayer within that relationship can make the difference between a church that comes through trouble stronger and a church that is weakened or even destroyed.

Prayer is learned behavior. Many people in our churches have fairly weak experiences of prayer because they have never been taught to pray beyond the level of "Now I lay me down to sleep. . . ."

This is tragic because God has chosen prayer as the means through which we are given what we need to do God's work and to be God's people. Weak praying makes for spiritually vulnerable churches. The basic pattern of spiritual provision that Jesus taught is that we ask and God gives. Persevering and believing prayer means a strong and abundant life in the church.

However, teaching people forms and practices of prayer alone will do little good without also working to strengthen the congregation's level of surrender and commitment to God. Prayer is not magic—using ritual words and actions to influence spiritual powers. Christian prayer is about relationship with God. It is about learning to trust that the God who created us loves us and wants to give us everything we need to live and be faithful. As we go out into the world, prayer puts our faith to work for God's glory and the good of others. Sailboat churches are on an adventure with God in the world, and prayer is the heartbeat of this adventure. Prayer takes our need, sins, joys, and thanksgivings to God as a little child takes the same to her parents. Prayer listens to God's direction and claims God's promises. Scripture is full of stories of people who trusted God in this way, prayed their needs in faith, and found God's grace coming to meet them. The God they knew is the same one who calls us into deeper relationship and fuller commitment.

The adventure God calls us into is at its heart a communal one. It is not enough that individual Christians pray by themselves. It is part of God's plan that we join together in praying congregations, and Christ promises to be with us in power when "two or three gather together in my name" (Matt. 18:20). Consistent teaching about prayer and opportunities to experience it are key to helping the whole congregation grow into a body that really acts together for God's sake. Sailboat churches offer special seasons of prayer, prayer retreats, and periodic meetings for prayer for special causes, such as peace and healing. Not everyone will take advantage of all these things, and some will never come, but as these opportunities are offered over the years, God will use them to build a culture of spiritual growth and empowerment in the congregation. Part of building a strong prayer foundation under the church is training believers to expect answers to prayer, recognize them when they come, and give thanks to God for them. The practice of testimony in the congregation is one way to do this. Hearing about what God has done in the life of another person encourages the rest of us and affirms the reality of faith. This, too, is something that can become part of the culture of the congregation, bringing a fresh wind of God's presence.

Every church should have at least one group of people who meet regularly to pray God's will for their congregation. Even a handful of folks who gather faithfully and expectantly to pray can open the door for God's transforming work. Pastors and lay leaders should be gathering regularly with these intentional groups to pray. Strong leadership should be exercised in these prayer groups to see that more time is spent praying than talking and that the groups stay mission/ministry focused rather than devolving into gossip centers. However, fear of these negative things should not block the church from experiencing the vitality that comes when the members gather regularly to pray.

All this spiritual preparation and growth in prayer needs to happen well before storms strike. It should be woven into the congregation's DNA. The Holy Spirit will use these practices to build a firm foundation under the church so that when troubles come, the resources will be there to meet them, and the congregation will be able to reap good spiritual fruit from the experience.

## Developing a Strong Leadership Team

Most Christian congregations have official lay leadership of some kind along with the services of a pastor. The powers and responsibilities of these lay leaders vary greatly from church to church, but lay leaders are a key component of the sailing team. In the best cases, the pastor(s) and the elected or appointed lay leaders function smoothly together as the spiritual leadership team of the church.

Having leaders who can work together well under the guidance of the Holy Spirit when trouble strikes is crucial to a church's health. However, high-functioning leadership teams don't just happen. Excellent leadership teams require an intentional commitment to recruit, train, resource, and encourage spiritual leaders. Once this commitment is made, the process begins with the leader selection or nominating process. In some ways, the team that nominates or selects lay leaders is the most important team in the church. It may even have as much long-term impact on the life of the congregation as the governing board does, because it nominates those who will be on the board. The stage for many an officer's good or not-so-good experience is set as the nominating committee does its job.

Of first importance is the question of how the committee understands the work it is elected to do. Its task is *not* simply to find people willing to fill slots on the ballot for officers! It is better to leave one or more positions unfilled for a while than to nominate someone who is unqualified or relunctant to serve. Rather, good nominating committees work on discerning both the congregation's leadership needs and the members who have the wherewithal to meet those needs. The person leading the selection or nominating process should make sure that a portion of the first meeting is given over to explaining the importance and spiritual focus of the committee's work. At this point the pastor can also give helpful theological and biblical grounding about discerning the call to spiritual leadership and recognizing spiritual gifts and talents that the church needs.

Wrapping prayer into every stage of the nominating committee's work enables the committee to keep its focus on doing God's work and also open doors for God's grace to flow into the whole process. Members of the committee can be urged to pray through the church membership directory as part of their preparation. Beyond opening and closing meetings with prayer, it is also helpful to take time out during the meetings at various points to pray for God's guidance. Visits and phone calls to prospective officers should be surrounded with prayer. Think about recruiting a small prayer team of church members who will support the work of the selection process. The congregation should be encouraged each week in worship and whenever church-wide concerns are shared to remember the work of the nominating or selection committee in its prayers.

After the lay leaders are elected or appointed, significant time should be spent training them for their calling. To put someone into the role of church officer without adequate training and support is to invite him or her to commit malpractice in spiritual leadership. After all, important parts of the congregation's life are being placed into that person's hands. With the pastor, the lay leaders are responsible for the health and growth of the congregation.

A basic officer training course should include, first, an exploration of an officer-elect's faith journey. The officers-elect should be helped to develop the ability to state their beliefs and give witness to how God has made a difference in their life. An introduction to church history gives officers a sense of spiritual roots and a reminder that they are not the first Christians who ever lived. Basic training in the congregation's particular beliefs and form of church government is essential. Lay leaders should also be led to a deep understanding of what their congregation's mission is, how decisions are made, and how they are expected to function in relation to the pastor and other leaders. If an officer-elect is responsible for particular church work or a committee, orientation should be provided.

This training time is also an opportunity for pastors to begin to build strong personal and working relationship with officers. These relationships lay the foundation for trust, good communication, and effective team work in the future. When trouble or conflict arises, officers and pastors will find that time spent in building trust and mutual understanding was well spent. Investing in training and building relationships with lay leaders is one of the best investments a pastor can make in the health of his or her congregation.

Once the new lay leaders are trained and in place, the pastor has a significant part to play in creating a good climate for team ministry. Pastors who see themselves a part of a team with the lay officers can use this team concept in sermons, prayers, announcements, and conversations with church members. Making decisions through the process of communal discernment when appropriate, rather than only discussion and voting, gives officers a chance to practice working together as a team. Practicing these things in ordinary times helps us perform better when trouble strikes. Communication between pastor and lay leaders is also key to good team work. Being the last to find out important information makes people feel unimportant and devalued. It also damages trust. Effective information-sharing does not just happen; it must be intentionally woven into the life of the church.

Another factor in the development of laypersons as members of the church's spiritual leadership team is the degree to which they receive personal support and spiritual care and counsel along the way, especially when they face difficulties. One of the causes of burnout among church officers is a combination of trouble at work or at home combined with a challenging situation at church. Pastors and other pastoral caregivers can help by keeping in close personal touch with the church's officers and making sure they get encouragement and care when needed. Pastors may find that trying times are excellent opportunities to deepen relationships with officers and to offer spiritual guidance that deepens faith. When lay leaders find that they can count on support and assistance from their church, they are encouraged to serve through hard times and find that their faith and Christian character are strengthened.

Finally, those who bear the burdens of leadership especially need encouragement and appreciation. While the glory always goes to God, celebrating the good things that have been achieved encourages the faithful and is a witness to uninvolved people of the joy found in doing God's work. One of the most powerful encouragements a church can provide to its spiritual leaders is to be intentional and regular about thanking them for their service. One congregation assigned each ruling elder an "angel" from the congregation. This person committed to pray for the elder, to remember his or her birthday, and to make encouraging contacts on a regular basis. Other congregations hold "Leader Appreciation Days" every couple of years so that during a three-year term all leaders will experience such an occasion. Teachers can talk to the Sunday school classes about the work of the church's leaders and have the children make thank-you cards to give each leader. Even remembering to say to a leader, "I appreciate what you do" in the hallway at church is encouraging.

It is also important for pastors to express genuine appreciation for the service of the leaders (and vice versa!). A good investment of time is for the pastor or a member of the pastoral staff to have a personal visit at least annually with each leader. These visits should have no other agenda than asking, "How are you doing?" and expressing appreciation for her or his service. Leaders' birthdays are great occasions for such visits. Leaders likewise can encourage pastors by making sure they know they are valued for their work and for themselves. Feeling appreciated often makes us want to do more; feeling unappreciated can lead to discouragement and bitterness.

## Preparing for Conflict

Sometimes conflict arises from outside the church in the form of opposition, obstacles, and even persecution. More often, however, the most upsetting conflicts arise inside the church. It is possible for someone to be a minimally active member of a congregation and never encounter conflict in the church. They may come to worship regularly, attend Sunday school, and be a member of a small group but be oblivious to any discord within the body. But leaders come to know the church at a deeper level, and this knowledge includes knowing about friction, disagreement, and even open conflict. Sometimes conflict becomes congregation-wide. This can be very disillusioning for those who have very high ideals for the church.

The fact is that conflict is a natural part of human interaction, and where there are human beings there will be conflict. Further, conflict can be a very healthy thing. An honest, healthy difference of opinions can help us clarify values and make wiser decisions, considering a wide variety of options rather than just one. The wise practice is to expect conflict and to prepare to deal with it in healthy ways.

*Understand the Congregation's History with Conflict.* Before conflict or trouble strikes, it is good to do some research to shed light on the experience and values of the church on this subject. This would be an excellent thing for a new pastor to do, but such a conversation could also begin to give a governing board some helpful insights about church life. Try to analyze the last two or three occasions when there were differences in the church. What was the conflict about? How severe was the conflict? Were people involved beyond the congregation? How was it officially resolved, or is it still simmering? Did anyone leave the church because of it, and are there still lingering effects in the congregation? Can you identify common issues or patterns of behavior involved in recent conflicts? Let people express their anxieties about conflict, and try to get an idea of which areas of church life seem most conflict producing. After this information is gathered, constructive reflection on it can be centered on the question, "What can we learn from this experience that will help us deal with conflict better in the future?" This evaluation can help people see the need to face and manage conflict positively and assertively.

*Agree on Guidelines for Managing Conflict.* While conflict will tend to produce anxiety in people and in the congregation, having previously agreed on some guidelines for working through conflicts can lower that anxiety. Part of the scariness of conflict is that it can blow up without warning, leaving us immersed in negative feelings and actions. Knowing what the rules are helps ground us in something more positive that hurt feelings and righteous indignation. The ground rules for dealing with conflict should be agreed on and widely known by all leaders. Talking over the conflict-management process should be part of new officer training. The Holy Spirit moves in this process to help the church grow through hard times.

If no agreed-on process is in place for conflict management, why not let the leadership team study Scripture and use insights from this study to come up with its own list of rules for handling differences? Scripture contains many passages that show conflicts happening or that give advice as to how to react. These Bible passages studied in light of the church's history and hope for the future can produce guidance about forgiveness, listening, healing, respecting one another, and listening to the Holy Spirit in times of conflict. This way of writing a set of guidelines for dealing with differences helps create ownership of the guidelines by church leaders.

*Practice Catching Conflict Early.* Good sailors always have an eye out for bad weather. Likewise, effective church leaders often look over the flock to sense where conflict and trouble may be brewing. The purpose of this attentiveness is not to avoid conflict but rather to deal with it in a timely and constructive manner before it becomes toxic. Conflict will often start as a difference of opinion about something or as a problem to be solved. How will the church's money be accounted for? What kind of music will we have in worship? How will our church buildings be used? How do we allocate money between various causes? What duties of the pastor and other staff members have highest priority? At this stage, simply gathering key stakeholders together and having a problem-solving meeting may take care of things. Often, new solutions will emerge that no one had thought of, allowing a fresh wind of the Spirit to move the church forward.

*Keep Communication Open.* Nobody likes being blindsided by negative information or feeling that he or she is always the last to know what's going on. Neither is it a good thing when people sense that secrets are being kept in the church and that only some people know the truth. Toxic conflict thrives when trust is low and suspicion is high. While being careful to keep confidential matters confidential, leaders who want to avoid toxic conflict will do everything in their power to open up the avenues of communication, letting information and conversation flow freely in the church.

*Practice Honesty, Humility, and Forgiveness as Core Values.* One tendency of our fallen human nature is to hold grudges and hide our true feelings from others. This behavior leads to tension and trouble in the church. When expectations are not met, when feelings are hurt, when mistakes are made, too often church people nurse the hurt and let it fester until it explodes in a nasty interaction of some kind. Such grudges and poisonous interactions grieve the Holy Spirit and hamper the church's effectiveness. They create an atmosphere that drains leaders and drives people away.

The apostle Paul speaks in Ephesians about a kind of Christian community that is deeper than surface niceness, that can function in turmoil and handle anger without souring or breaking apart. "He knows that when real people live in real community with one another, they will discover real differences and suffer real discord. This is true whether the community is a marriage, a family, a neighborhood, a church, or the whole society. It is not possible to love one another without hating one another from time to time. When that time comes, Paul says, do not shut up and disappear. Speak the truth in love. Be angry but do not sin. 'Be kind to one another, tenderhearted, forgiving one another, as God in Christ has forgiven you'" (Eph. 4:32).[1]

It takes time to change a congregation's culture, but it must start somewhere and the most effective place is with the church's leaders. While preaching and teaching about the quality of life marks a Spirit-led congregation, leaders can also set godly standards for their own interactions with one another. As honest, humble, forgiving ways of acting take root in the leadership, chances are it will also leak out into the congregation.

## Cultivating Emotional Health

Churches sail more effectively when their members work together in harmonious unity. This unity is a gift of the Spirit. It comes when we desire and work for God's will above all things. At the same time, we can open up channels for this gift to flow by practicing healthy ways of relating to our fellow sailors. Here are some practices that can help this to happen.[2]

*Foster Healthy Distance and Nonanxious Presence.* Most people tend to feel lonely and depressed when they do not have close relationships with others. At the same time, however, we also benefit from a certain amount of healthy distance in our relationships with others. When people are too emotionally attached to other people, they tend to react very strongly to whatever the others say or do, and this reaction can generate conflict. For instance, in some married couples, if the wife becomes depressed, the husband also becomes depressed; so instead of his being an encouraging presence for her, they both spiral down into depression together. Or if the husband gets angry, even though what he is angry about has nothing to do with her, the wife reacts by becoming irritable and defensive. Healthy distance means that each person has enough self-possession to be calm and helpful even when the other is angry, anxious, or depressed.

These same dynamics come into play in church life. A church with too much togetherness can be a very tense place. If one person is upset, the whole church can get upset. This dynamic is particularly hard on leaders. Since, in most churches, somebody is unhappy most of the time, being a leader can be very stressful. One way to deal with this tension is to practice being a nonanxious presence.

Picture Jesus sleeping through a raging storm in the bottom of the boat while his terrified disciples work to keep the boat from sinking (Mark 4:35–41). Jesus was able to stay calm in the presence of others' anxiety. This kind of calm is crucial in organizations; when people become highly anxious and emotional, their ability to solve problems logically decreases dramatically. Interactions between people devolve to the level of personalities, and conflicts become frequent.

Developing the ability to act as a nonanxious presence in a troubled church is, in part at least, a spiritual work. In order to be a nonanxious presence for others, we need to have one in our own lives. The ultimate source of spiritual peace is faith in a faithful God. Jesus did not need to go into a panic during the storm because he knew that his Abba (Father) had the situation under control. A well-nourished relationship with God and a sense that God is faithful gives leaders something to stand on in a crisis.

*Spread the Work Around.* In a healthy church, work is shared among many members, with each doing his or her job. Sometimes, however, churches slip into a situation where some people do much more than their share. Taking responsibility for tasks others should be doing has been called "overfunctioning."

Here's an example: the grounds chairman goes out late Saturday afternoon to cut the church lawn. He does this because the person who has been assigned this job hasn't done it or hasn't done it to the chairman's specifications. Cutting the lawn himself means that he does not have to confront directly the person who was supposed to mow. Also, he doesn't have to listen to members complain the next day about how bad the lawn looks. However, this behavior has a cost. The chairman resents having to mow the lawn, and he goes to church the next day feeling put upon and burdened. Doing too much is not good for the individual or for the church and can lead to all kinds of problems.

Overfunctioning by some creates a situation where others tend to underfunction. If the Christian education committee chair does all the recruiting of Sunday school teachers rather than asking the rest of the committee to help, she is teaching the committee that recruiting is the chair's responsibility. This sets up a pattern for the future. The leader's willingness to do too much enables others to feel comfortable doing too little.

Further, a person can experience spiritual fallout from doing too much. The joy and blessing that can come from serving God is sapped out of church work when it is done out of anxiety or the feeling that "I have to do it or it won't get done." It becomes a heavy burden and will sooner or later wear people out. They may lose their sense of relationship with God altogether, and only a lifeless sense of duty keeps them going.

People in small-membership congregations can be particularly at risk for overfunctioning.

Over the years, churches tend to acquire all kinds of activities and functions that taken together constitute "what our church does." All these activities and functions require effort on the part of people to keep them going. Letting any of them go may seem like failure. In this situation, some people begin to take on the duties of people who are no longer in the church or have become disabled.

One way to avoid this danger is to practice regular periods of evaluation and elimination of activities that cannot be carried on without overburdening people. If there is no one to run the annual men's barbecue, for instance, perhaps this means that the barbecue is not as important as it used to be. If the barbecue is discontinued, there might be energy in the church for a new activity to emerge, giving new life to the congregation and opening the way for new people to get involved in the church's life.

*Avoid Emotional Triangles.* When two people or groups of people feel uncomfortable with each other and don't want to confront a problem directly, they will often bring in a third party to help them feel better. This reaction has been called "triangling." Whenever a person gets emotionally involved with what is essentially someone else's issue, a triangle is probably in the making.

For instance, when the pastor who feels underpaid complains to the church secretary about how unappreciative and stingy the congregation is, the pastor is triangling the secretary into what is essentially a matter the pastor needs to resolve with the church's governing board or congregation. She does this because it is easier to vent to the secretary and get it off her chest than it is to confront others with her desire for a raise. The secretary may feel honored to be the one the pastor talks to about her dissatisfaction and may encourage more of it. On the pastor's side, this "it's us against the congregation" venting may provide enough emotional relief that the pastor never gets up the courage to ask for a raise. Triangling is spiritually and emotionally unhealthy. It allows problems to fester, poisoning relationships in the church.

Here is a situation where a church member turns simmering conflict in a healthier direction. Maria Jones goes to visit Mrs. Sinclair, an elderly homebound member of the congregation. Mrs. Sinclair complains to Maria that the pastor does not come to see her as often as she feels he should. She talks about how frustrated she is with the pastor's sermons, which she listens to on tape, and bemoans the fact that, "This new pastor is not half the man our last pastor was." Maria asks Mrs. Sinclair if she has ever voiced her concerns to the pastor personally, but the elderly woman is shocked and says she would never think of such a thing. Instead she continues to pour criticism into the ears of the deacon for the next half hour.

Maria leaves this visit resolving to pray for guidance about the problem of Mrs. Sinclair's negative relationship with the new pastor. After doing so, two weeks later she makes an appointment to talk with the pastor. In her conversation with him, she focuses not on Mrs. Sinclair's specific grievances but rather on the close relationship the homebound member had with the last pastor and Maria's sense of her need to feel connected with the new pastor. The pastor responds by promising to visit Mrs. Sinclair and to try to get to know her better. Maria warns him to be prepared for a possible chilly reception at first, but they both agree that it was worth the effort to reach out to a lonely homebound member in this way. Mrs. Sinclair receives the pastor's visit with guarded warmth. Over time, they develop such a positive relationship that Mrs. Sinclair tells him she wants him to do her funeral with the former pastor assisting. In working in this situation to bring Mrs. Sinclair and the pastor together, Maria works as a true peacemaker.

If the relationship between the pastor and Mrs. Sinclair had remained negative in spite of Maria's efforts, she would still need to avoid getting triangled into the middle of Mrs. Sinclair's negativity. It is important in such a situation to keep trying to get the people involved to work their problems out together. However, if those efforts do not succeed, Maria should set a firm boundary around this subject and not allow Mrs. Sinclair to use her as a dumping ground for her criticism of the pastor. She can say something like, "Mrs. Sinclair, I really enjoy visiting with you, but I am going to have to ask you not to share your criticisms of the pastor with me. It doesn't do either one of us really any good. I am happy to talk with you about anything but that."

❧ ❧ ❧ ❧ ❧ ❧ ❧

Having done all these things to prepare, remember that conflict is part of normal human interaction and nothing to be ashamed of in the church or elsewhere. Healthy churches recognize and name problems before the atmosphere around them becomes too emotional or personalized. They claim the presence and gifts of the Spirit to face them openly, honestly, and prayerfully. This way of dealing with conflict brings glory to God and adds to the health of the church and its effectiveness for mission.

## Questions for Reflection

1. Some people believe that there should be no conflict in religious organizations. Why do you think this is? Is conflict at church more disturbing than conflict at home or at work? Why?
2. Think about the last conflict your congregation experienced. What positive outcomes emerged from it?
3. How effective is your church's leadership nomination process? In what ways could it be improved?
4. How do you personally react to conflict situations? What spiritual resources can you draw on to deal with conflict in graceful ways?
5. Has anyone ever attempted to "triangle" you? How did you react?

Chapter 10

# Navigation

*W*hen a Sailboat leaves the harbor and goes to sea, navigation comes into play. This ancient skill involves charting a passage between where the boat is and where it needs to go. Similarly, with the help of the Holy Spirit, Sailboat churches are called to navigate into God's will in their mission and ministry. This involves a way of life marked by discernment.

## What Is Discernment?

Christian discernment involves making choices that draw us more toward God's will than away from it. Discernment is important because being Christian is not simply about subscribing to a set of doctrines or religious beliefs. The essence of Christianity is the call to be a disciple, a follower of Jesus Christ. It is a call to a Christ-like way of life, and this way of life involves choosing to do some things and not to do others.

Not every choice in life or in the church requires an intentional process of discernment. Many choices are guided by fixed commitments, routine, common sense, or discernments made on similar situations in the past. We don't generally pause and discern whether or not to stop the car at a stop sign or what to have for lunch or whether to pick the kids up from school. At church, we make many decisions about routine matters by common consent because there is a common understanding about what God requires.

When God's will is not clear, however, we must work to understand it. An intentional process of discernment is most appropriate when the matter at hand has significant, long-term consequences, when there are different views on the subject or a variety of choices to be considered, and when the circumstances allow time for working through the matter instead of requiring a quick decision.

Discernment, however, is not primarily a technique for making big decisions. It is a way of orienting ourselves toward God as the true north of our lives. It develops in us a Christian character. As with all spiritual practices, the goal of discernment is that little by little we come to embody the gospel and become obedient partners in God's work in the world.

As believers live into this reality in their personal lives, the transforming influence of the Holy Spirit will also change how they do business at church. The opposite flow can also take place. Those who engage in intentionally seeking God's will in the congregation can find that this way of being begins to transform the rest of their lives. The New Testament speaks of this transformation in terms of having our minds set on the Spirit (Rom. 8:5), living by the Spirit and being led by the Spirit (Gal. 5:16–17), and bearing the image of the "man of heaven" ("Christ"; 1 Cor. 15:49).

Other Scriptures speak in communal terms of the whole Christian community being transformed. In Romans 12:1–2, the writer uses Greek plural pronouns (you all) to encourage the entire church not to be conformed to this world. Instead, they are urged to allow themselves to be transformed by the renewing of their minds as they daily offer their bodies as living sacrifices.

People who are being transformed in this way will be:

*God-focused and obedient.* The key questions of discernment are: What is God's call to us? What is God's desire in this situation? What is God doing, and how can we join in? In asking these questions, we assume that God will make God's desire known to us as we pray, listen, and search. The God that Jesus showed us is a God eager to be known. Jesus urged his disciples to ask, seek, and knock, assuring them that by God's grace prayers offered in his name will be answered.

Discernment also brings us face to face with the call to surrender ourselves fully to God. We can partner with God in God's work only to the degree that we are willing to be obedient. We must let God take the lead and do what only God can do. Too often, we assume we know what God wants, and we set out to do it with perhaps a little prayer for God to help us. This approach may stir up a whirlwind of activity, engage numbers of people in programs, and even do some good in the world. However, these efforts usually bear little lasting fruit. Practicing discernment reminds us that every day we are first and foremost to be about the task of seeking God's will, not our own.

One of the beautiful things about a discerning way of life is that it keeps us expectantly turned toward God. It relieves us of the tyranny of circumstances, the obsession with personalities and politics, and the addiction to always have our way. Instead, we all turn as one to face the One who promises to lead us if we are willing to be led.

There are times when discernment can test our faith. Sometimes the guidance we have prayed for leads us on a course that does not seem reasonable. The writer of Proverbs calls on the people to "Trust in the Lord with all your heart and do not rely on your own insight. In all your ways acknowledge him, and he will make straight your paths" (3:5–6). A discerning way of life teaches us to trust God beyond that which we can see. It can challenge us to follow where God seems to be pointing even when we cannot see the way ahead. If we take up discernment as our way of life, we must be aware that we may be led outside our comfort zones and involved in actions that, at the time, may make little sense on a strictly logical level.

*Spirit-led.* At the center of the practice of discernment is the experience of God's Spirit leading us as we seek God's will. Jesus stressed God's readiness to help believers by promising, "If you then, who are evil [sinful], know how to give good gifts to your children, how much more will the heavenly Father give the Holy Spirit to those who ask" (Luke 11:13). True Christian discernment can happen only as we claim Jesus' promise and open ourselves to the Holy Spirit's work in our midst. This openness requires the humility to let go of our desires so that we might be open to God's desire, whatever that may turn out to be.

We must be very careful not to fall into thinking of the Holy Spirit as a means to our ends, no matter how good those ends might be. The Spirit is not a religious tool that we use to grow our church or get something done for God. Instead, the Holy Spirit uses us to the end that God's will is done on earth as it is in heaven. The degree to which we are willing to become servants of the Spirit is the degree to which God can use us.

*Communal.* Having the humility to seek guidance from others is essential to the discerning way of life. This is because the Holy Spirit often sends us spiritual guidance through other people. As groups discuss and pray, insight will often come through the minds and spirits of the group members. Discernment requires that we honor the contributions of others and listen for God's truth to come from them even though we may disagree with some of what they say.

There are also special people in every community of faith who have unusually deep insights into the things of God. Steeped in prayer, grounded in Scripture, and gifted with wisdom from the Holy Spirit, these people are great resources in times of discernment. Likewise, we can be guided by the wisdom of people we have met only indirectly through books, articles, printed or recorded lectures, or sermons. Sometimes an image, a story, or even a single word will open the way forward.

## What Does "God's Will" Mean?

As we explore the idea of a discerning life, some may wonder: Can we actually know God's particular will in any given situation? What about all the evil that has been done through the centuries by people who thought they were doing God's will? How can we be sure we are doing God's will and not our own? Many volumes of theology have been written on these questions, and I do not intend to write another one here. However, if we desire a discerning way of life, it is important to have a basic working understanding of what we mean by the phrase "God's will."

At the heart of this concept is the truth that God cares about what we do. Our choices matter to God because we, both individuals and communities, matter to God. God loves us, and that love has been expressed in its highest form in Jesus Christ. By his life and death he showed us God's love and fulfilled God's will in everything he did and said. Christians are called to let our actions be shaped on a daily basis both by the witness to Christ that we have in Scripture and by the living presence of his Holy Spirit.

Finding God's will is not a game of hide-and-seek with God hiding and us seeking. The truth is that we already know more of God's will than we are often willing to carry out. We know that it is God's will that we love our enemies, turn the other cheek when attacked, forgive and pray for those who injure us, and reject opportunities for revenge. We know it is God's will that we live a moderate, healthful, modest life, being good stewards of our bodies because they are temples of the Holy Spirit. These precepts and many others like them are stated in the Bible.

Discipleship involves attuning ourselves day by day to God's will as we find it in Scripture and as we are led into it by God's Spirit in our daily lives. More than anything else, this daily struggle to make Christ-like choices and to order our communities in line with God's will shapes us into discerning people. As we grow in our desire to serve and glorify God, we are empowered by the Holy Spirit.

Those who practice this daily discipline come into the process of communal decision making, such as a church committee or board meeting, equipped to listen for God's will for the church. They know the voice of God in the "sound of sheer silence" (1 Kgs. 19:12). Gathered as the people of God, they test all discernments by God's perfect word: Jesus Christ as revealed in Scripture and interpreted by the Holy Spirit.

When faced with discernment around a particular issue, many well-intentioned Christians are paralyzed by the fear of making a mistake. Underlying this fear may be the idea that God's will is like a bull's-eye on a target, and, in order to please God, we have to hit it perfectly. Maybe it is better to refuse to engage in discernment than to risk getting the wrong answer. Psalm 103 provides a healthy corrective: "As a father has compassion for his children, so the LORD has compassion for those who fear him. For he knows how we were made; he remembers that we are dust" (Ps. 103:13–14). God does not expect perfection. God expects us to do our best to live as faithful disciples. God knows that our choices and actions will often be flawed because we are flawed creatures. But God is also delighted by our attempts to know and do his will and, like a loving parent, has mercy on our failures.

In thinking about God's will, it is also helpful to remember that God is already at work in the world in ways too numerous to count. Instead of hitting the bull's-eye, perhaps seeking God's will means listening to the sounds and signs of God at work in the world and being willing to get in the flow of what God is already doing. Why not think of it as finding where the rivers of God's will are already flowing in the world and jumping in?

This is an image of commitment and faith. To enter a river means that we will not stay in the same place. As the river flows along, sometimes the ride will be placid, sometimes it will be rough. Our task is not to direct the river or make it flow, but rather to take our place in the current. While far from a perfect image for seeking God's will, it does capture the truth that discernment of God's call, in our own lives and at church, is an ongoing way of life. It reminds us that we are engaged in a process that God is directing. This way of understanding God's will requires more from us than an exercise in hitting the bull's-eye from time to time when important matters arise. When Christians make the commitment to stay in the flow of God's will no matter where it leads, church becomes an adventure!

## The Art of Listening

As we commit ourselves to this adventure, the first challenge before us is slowing down and waiting quietly to hear the still, small voice of the Holy Spirit. Without learning to listen for the Spirit's guidance we cannot navigate. It is often a challenge to hear the Spirit speak. We are surrounded by a babble of other voices seeking our attention. Part of our obedience to God comes in creating space in our personal lives and in our life together for the Spirit to encourage, direct, convict, teach, and equip us. This practice is especially important for leaders. The soul-full leader is faithful to the one thing he can do—create the conditions that set us up for an encounter with God where we need it most. In attentive, obedient openness to God, we will be given direction and resources to meet the challenge before us.

Many congregations are desperate for answers and direction as they face the challenges of our time. The truth is that there is no reliable direction apart from listening to the One who is the Lord of the church. Instead of doing the hard work of learning to navigate through listening to God's voice, we are tempted to seize on quick fixes. The prophet Isaiah warned the Israelites against such behavior when they were threatened by enemies.

> "Woe to the obstinate children,"
>     declares the LORD,
> "to those who carry out plans that are not mine,
>     forming an alliance, but not by my Spirit, . . .
> who go down to Egypt
>     without consulting me;
> who look for help to Pharaoh's protection, . . .
> These are rebellious people, deceitful children,
>     children unwilling to listen to the LORD's instruction. . . ."
> "In repentance and rest is your salvation,
>     in quietness and trust is your strength."
>                         (Isa. 30:1–2, 9, 15 NIV)

Human-devised strategies to save the church are just as obnoxious to God today as they were in Isaiah's time. Becoming discerning navigators requires that we turn first to God and God alone as the source of our help. Doing this requires us to practice listening, rest, humility, and trust. These things may seem ridiculous and even irresponsible in times of trouble. The urge to fix things by depending on our wisdom and resources is strong, especially for those who are in leadership roles.

When the storms are raging or we feel we have lost our way, when the crew is not unified, or when the territory we have come into is completely unfamiliar, the last thing that seems appropriate is resting or slowing down. Rather we get busy, start rowing frantically, and often end up making decisions and plans that are not rooted in God. Instead of leading out of rest, stillness, and trust we end up leading out of weariness and compulsive activity. As we repent of our self-generated agendas and plans, inviting God to be at the center of our lives, we will be enabled to be most faithful and most effective.

As we begin praying for God to lead us, in faith we make space in our lives where we can intentionally listen for God. Most people in this process will want to find a way to spend time with God regularly. Providing encouragement and resources for this practice is important in Sailboat churches. This is where the teaching ministry of the church is crucial. Many people are hungry to receive God's guidance but have no idea how to go about listening to God. We can equip believers to listen for the still, small voice through

- teaching various ways of listening to God in prayer
- helping people reflect on their own life experiences and events in the wider world in light of Scripture
- helping people listen for God more effectively in sacraments, liturgy, music, sermons, art, and spiritual readings
- finding ways to listen to God in committees, business, and planning meetings
- teaching how to be silent and receptive in God's presence
- offering opportunities to meet with spiritual friends or mentors
- organizing and resourcing small groups of people who want to grow closer to God
- teaching the skills of discernment as a way to make decisions in church governing bodies
- planning retreats that help people carve out time to experience God's speaking to them

This list barely scratches the surface of how we can assist people in their desire to hear God's voice. It is important to remember while helping people learn to listen that what works for one person may not work for another. A variety of settings and methods should be offered.

## Discerning the *Kairos* Moments

Timing is always a factor in discernment. Biblical Greek has two words that are translated into English as the word *time*. One is *chronos*, indicating time as measured by a clock or calendar. This kind of time governs when we get up in the morning and go to bed at night. We pick up the children from school and show up for our doctors' appointments at certain times. *Chronos* is what we live our lives by day in and day out. However, the Bible also talks about another kind of time that in Greek is called *kairos*. This word refers to a special season of life when certain actions are appropriate or to a time of exceptional opportunity from God.

Effective spiritual leaders will develop sensitivity to these *kairos* moments, the spiritual times and seasons in the life of the church. The writer of Ecclesiastes says, "For everything there is a season, and a time for every matter under heaven" (Eccl. 3:1), and then catalogs a variety of things in life that each have a special time. The idea here is that certain activities are appropriate at certain seasons or times and others are not. If the church has suffered many losses, it may be the season to grieve. If a new building has been built or the church is commemorating a major anniversary, it will be time to celebrate. There are times when the church needs to draw inward and pay close attention to its communal life. Then there are times when it is appropriate to focus major energy in mission outside the congregation. The context gives leaders clues about what is appropriate for a particular time in the church's life. God has particular challenges and opportunities for a congregation in each *kairos* season.

Timing is also extremely important in bringing to birth new programs and ministries in the church. Those who have delivered children into the world can testify that there is a time to let nature take its course and then there is a time to push. Pushing too soon can injure the baby. So it is also in trying to bring something new into the life of the church. There are seasons when proposals need to germinate in the minds and hearts of people. There are times to move plans along slowly, allowing everyone to get on board. And then there are times to act swiftly and decisively to push it on through into fulfillment. Effective spiritual leadership involves sensing when to push and when to hold back.

Another facet of the meaning of *kairos* refers to that special, holy time when God presents human beings with an exceptional opportunity. The first words out of Jesus' mouth in the Gospel of Mark are, "The time is fulfilled, and the kingdom of God has come near; repent, and believe the good news" (1:15). Jesus' presence among us on earth was the ultimate *kairos* moment. He held the door of God's kingdom open, and people were obliged either to enter or to turn away. There is no place for neutrality when such times come.

Jesus shows us the impact *kairos* moments have on people in two familiar parables in Matthew. One man finds a hidden treasure in a field, "then in his joy he goes and sells all he has and buys that field" (13:44). Another man, a pearl merchant, "on finding one pearl of great value, . . . went and sold all that he had and bought it" (13:45,46). The kingdom of heaven, Jesus says, is like these amazing surprises. It fills us with joy and excitement; it may also require us to take significant risks and to sacrifice everything.

Another factor involved in discerning *kairos* moments is the willingness to wait on God. Human nature loves to rush things to conclusion. We are disappointed if our projects go slowly or involve waiting. Sailors know that there are times when the wind stops blowing temporarily. In our Sailboat church, too, there are times when we seem becalmed. The call during times like these is twofold.

First, we wait patiently and humbly for God to do what only God can do. It may be that God is waiting for us to be prepared for the answer to our prayers. Waiting humbles us to realize that God is the senior partner, the One in control of things. Our job is to come into line with whatever God is up to. It may be that we are not ready for the vision to become a reality yet. Some work may need to be done in us before God can go further. Or perhaps God is testing us to see if we are willing to release our dream, leaving it on the altar of obedience. When it seems the wind has stopped blowing, often the best thing we can do is to let go of the work and spend more time seeking and listening to God.

Second, we keep our eyes and spiritual intuition alert to see where the Spirit may be moving. When the wind dies down at sea, sailors look around to see where the surface of the water is ruffled. That is a sign that the wind is blowing nearby. When we are spiritually becalmed, we also can take up the watch for signs of the Spirit at work around us in ways we might not have imagined. When we find our life or our church in the doldrums, the temptation is to whip up activity and distraction. Wise sailors resist this temptation and instead go deeper into prayer, asking for eyes to see and ears to hear how the Spirit wants to lead them in the situation.

*Test What Is Heard.* Not everything that we hear when we listen is from God. Just as important as listening is the process of testing what we hear. The evaluation of particular discernments requires a deep sense of what it entails to be Jesus' disciples and an understanding of what Christian faithfulness means. Questions that arise include: Does the discernment bear the marks of Jesus, the suffering servant?

Does it take us out of our comfort zones to follow Jesus? Does it seem to accord with God's desires for healing and salvation in this world? Does it call us to deny self? Answering these kinds of questions requires a firm grounding in Scripture. It is not so important to be able to quote reams of Scripture from memory. Rather our goal is to be so steeped in the full witness of Scripture that it shapes how we think, what we want, and how we relate to God and others. Instead of using Scripture to further our ends, we must have the humility to let Scripture judge, direct, and transform us.

Some traditions have generally agreed on lists of confessional documents that help them test individual and corporate discernments. These documents remind us that others before us have wrestled with the demands of the gospel and left us their testimony. These voices from the past help us understand what true faithfulness may look like in our day. The resources may include the operational documents and by-laws of denominations and congregations. They represent the distilled wisdom of the community regarding how the church should operate.

Along with prayerfully consulting Scripture and tradition, discussing the matter with wise fellow believers can help us test our discernments. Those who take discernment as their life path will find it helpful to have a spiritual friend, mentor, or prayer partner to consult with regularly. It is humbling to submit our understanding of what God has said to others for their response. Being ready to do this, however, is a sign that we really do want God's will and only God's will.

Finally, in the long term, discernment can be tested by the fruit that it bears. Over time, does the decision made tend to enhance the health and mission of the church? Does it seem to draw us closer to God? Do we see more fruit of the Spirit—love, joy, peace, patience, kindness, meekness, faithfulness, gentleness, and self control (Gal. 5:22–23)—growing in ourselves or the church as a result of the decision? Does it help us reach out beyond the walls of the church to draw others to God? Underneath the surface emotions generated by change and circumstance, is there a sense of peace when the decision is carried out? These and similar questions help us learn from our discernments and equip us for deeper faithfulness in the future.

## A Story of Spiritual Navigation

What does this discerning life really look like in a congregation? The following account by a pastor shows some of its postures and moves.

"Last summer we were scheduled to go down to work with our sister church in Mexico City. As the trip was coming together, I had a nagging sense that I, or we, were not supposed to go. There were a number of factors involved other than my own unsettled feeling: the sign-ups were lower than usual, people kept saying no, a few even said they did not feel called to go.

I was conflicted about going. On the one hand, I had a feeling something was not right. On the other hand, there would be so many people I would be disappointing if we did not go. Also God had used my experiences in Mexico with our church teams to speak powerful and transformative truths in my life.

In the midst of all this, I got an email from the woman in our church who was going to help lead the trip saying she had filled out the application on the computer but just could not hit *send* and email it to me. She had been praying and felt as though she was not supposed to go. I was devastated and frustrated. There would be so many people I would be disappointing if we did not go. Soon after this I met with my spiritual director. We discussed the situation. At one point she asked me, "Have you given yourself permission not to go?" I began to weep! I realized that because of the heavy obligation I felt to go, I had not been open in my spirit to letting the trip drop. This was a powerful and freeing insight for me.

I asked our staff and some key leaders to begin to pray about what we should do. One of our staff had an image of an empty field come into her mind while we were praying and asking the Lord for discernment. We were not exactly sure what that meant, but it became an important anchor to our journey.

There were numerous indicators leading us to not go to Mexico, but the confirmation came when I called the pastor of our sister church in Mexico City. I told him we felt the Lord was prompting us to take a year of rest from coming down to be with them this year. I was filled with fear and waited with anxiety and dread for his response. The pastor said, "We will join in prayer but, if God is leading you to not come this year, then we don't want you to disobey his will and come!" Immediately peace began to wash over me.

After we discerned not going to Mexico was God's leading, more and more began to be shown to us. We received guidance to slow down and focus on the things we were already doing in our own neighborhood. That summer we organized four peace vigils for teenagers shot in our community, and we had many volunteers serve at our church's urban farm. We invested time to develop deeper friendships with our sister African American church. And we did all this out of a place of quietness, rest, and trust instead of constrained and distracted activity.

We could have willfully pushed through our misgivings and gone to Mexico out of a sense of obligation. Instead, the culture in our congregation of slowing down to discern allowed us to keep in step with the Spirit. We stopped to listen, we heard God's direction, and we obeyed."

≻ ≻ ≻ ≻ ≻ ≻ ≻

God's promise to the Israelites is also God's promise to us today: "And when you turn to the right or when you turn to the left, your ears shall hear a word behind you saying, 'This is the way; walk in it'" (Isa. 30:21). Spiritual navigation is the process of listening for that voice so that we can be obedient. The way forward is discerned as we listen to God together.

## Questions for Reflection

1. How would you define "God's will" to a thirteen-year-old member of the confirmation class?
2. What is one area of your life in which the choices you make and have made are largely determined by what you believe to be God's will? How have your beliefs about God's will shaped your choices?
3. How do you experience the power of the Holy Spirit at work in your life?
4. This chapter mentions images of hitting a bull's-eye and jumping in a river as ways to understanding what it means to do God's will. Which of these images is more helpful to you and why?

5. According to the book of Acts, the early church was guided and empowered by God, specifically through the actions of the Holy Spirit. What areas of your church's life could benefit from some empowering by the Holy Spirit?

# Conclusion

$S$ome years ago I was traveling around the country on behalf of my denomination. Part of this trip involved visiting a number of churches in small towns across the state of Nebraska. Many of these towns were shrinking due to massive changes in agriculture over the last thirty years. Parcels of land that once supported a dozen families were now being farmed by one. The theme I heard over and over again during these visits went something like, "We can't do church now the way we have before."

For some of these congregations this was the end of the story. Not doing church like we have always done it before meant not doing church much longer. But then one day I heard something different in another small church that, on the surface, looked much like all the others. After repeating a similar tale of change and decline, one of the lay leaders said, "So we are asking God 'What do you want us to be doing now?'"

This question suggested to me that this little group was putting down the oars and putting up the sails. They knew that as long as there was a God interested in saving the world there would always be work for the church. It might not look much like anything they had done before. It might lead them far outside their comfort zones. But they were expecting God to answer their prayer for guidance, fill their sails, and move them on into the future. They did not have much, but they were putting themselves into God's hands and waiting expectantly to see what God would do.

When we exhaust everything in our bag of tricks and the church is still languishing or sinking, there is a way forward. God is yearning to ignite us with all the passion and power we need for the work of our mission fields. We have hardly scratched the surface of the divine resources that are available to us. Why not put up the sails and see what God can do?

Blessed sailing to you!

# Guide to Forty Days of Prayer

*I*f a church is to sail, there must be a critical mass of people who are willing to become sailors. Only God can make the changes in our life that will turn those of us who are by nature rowers into sailors. However, sailing begins with praying. Participating in interactive prayer puts us where the Holy Spirit can make us into sailors. This prayer guide is offered as a starting place for that process.

Begin each day's exercise by asking God to open your mind and heart to what God wants to do in you. Read the Scripture several times and think about what it says. Then read the section "Listening to God" and meditate on what God might be saying to you personally. Next, pray your response to God from your listening and meditation. Writing your prayer down will give you something to reflect on later. However you pray, make the prayer as honest and personal as you can. Trust God to meet you where you are and give you what you need.

Let these readings and reflections lead you into deeper intimacy with God. After you have gone through the forty days, gather a small group to go through it again together with you. This could be done in conjunction with reading and discussing one of the books in the "Readings for Further Exploration" section. If this seems to be bearing fruit, think about using the prayer guide in your church in classes, small groups, or a church-wide season of prayer.

# Day One

**Scripture:** Jeremiah 29:1–14

**Focus Text:** "When you search for me, you will find me; if you seek me with all your heart, I will let you find me, says the LORD" (vv. 13–14).

**Listening to God:** When was the last time you really searched for me? Your days are full of other things that compete for your time and attention, but I am the only one who loves you unconditionally and forever. I hold everything in my hands. So much of what you worry about I have already taken care of for you. It will work out. Today, set aside some time to let me bless you with a deeper sense of my presence.

**My Prayer:**

# Day Two

**Scripture:** Lamentation 3:22–33

**Focus Text:** "It is good that one should wait quietly for the salvation of the LORD" (v. 26).

**Listening to God**: I am a God who loves to save. I like nothing more than bringing my Spirit and my healing into your life. Please give me more room to operate! When you thrash around in complaint and impatience you block my blessings. Take a deep breath and give me time to complete the growth I am trying to bring about in your soul.

**My Prayer:**

# Day Three

**Scripture:** Psalm 42:1–11

**Focus Text:** "As the deer longs for flowing streams, so my soul longs for you, O God" (v. 1).

**Listening to God:** The desire you feel for me is put into your heart by the Holy Spirit. Rejoice in this desire! Hold onto it like a lifeline. Your yearning for me is a sign that my love has been poured into your heart by faith. Your thirst for me draws you closer and closer to me so that I can claim more and more of you. I am using your desire, as unfulfilled and frustrating as it may feel, to transform you into the person I want you to be.

**My Prayer:**

# Day Four

**Scripture:** Acts 17:16–33

**Focus Text:** "Indeed he is not far from each one of us. For 'In him we live and move and have our being'"(vv. 27–28).

**Listening to God**: Know that right at this moment, I am very close to you. The air that you are breathing is a gift from me. The ability to turn a page or read a sentence comes to you right now from my loving hands. It grieves me when you act as though I am far away. You give me great joy when you recognize our intimacy and live like a son or daughter of God. I desire your good as a mother desires good for her infant. Trust me and don't be afraid!

**My Prayer**:

## Day Five

**Scripture:** Matthew 5:1–16

**Focus Text**: "Blessed are the poor in spirit, for theirs is the kingdom of heaven" (v. 3).

**Listening to God**: I desire fellowship with you more than anything else in the universe. You often expect me to bless you most in your abundance. This is not the way I work. When I bless you in your abundance, you tend to forget me in fascination with my gifts. The gifts become an idol, and our relationship suffers. It is my way to bless you in your lack, failure, and emptiness. This way you don't forget me, and I can work my will through you in amazing ways. Look for my hand moving in your life when you are feeling lonely, incompetent, and out of control. Blessed are you when you don't run away from the means I use to draw you to me.

**My Prayer**:

# Day Six

**Scripture:** Psalm 34

**Focus Text:** The LORD is near to the brokenhearted, and saves the crushed in spirit" (v. 18).

**Listening to God**: It is sad that you often feel my presence least when you are in the most need. It should be just the opposite. Like any good parent, my love reaches its peak when my child needs help. I have everything you need and want to give it to you. All you have to do is ask. Repent your lack of trust and come to me in prayer. I will bring good out of anything that is tormenting you.

**My Prayer:**

# Day Seven

**Scripture:** Mark 1:14–20

**Focus Text:** "The time is fulfilled, and the kingdom of God has come near; repent, and believe in the good news" (v. 15).

**Listening to God:** I want to do something new in you and in your church. This new thing is of a piece with what I have been doing with you, but it is also fresh and different. I want you to turn away from your contentment with the way things are and ask me what I want you to be doing. I want you to partner with me now, not next week or next year. There are people all around you who need what only I can give. Let me use you to be good news to them.

**My Prayer:**

# Day Eight

**Scripture:** Luke 15:11–24

**Focus Text:** "While he was still far off, his father saw him and was filled with compassion; he ran and put his arms around him and kissed him" (v. 20).

**Listening to God:** Your unfaithfulness does not change my faithfulness to you. Your sin does not erase our relationship. Jesus died on a cross so that sin would not have the last word between us. Turn and take one step in my direction, and I will run to meet you. You cannot imagine how the angels rejoice when they see you turn for home.

**My Prayer:**

# Day Nine

**Scripture:** Revelation 2:1–7

**Focus Text:** "I have this against you, that you have abandoned the love you had at first" (v. 4).

**Listening to God:** Haven't you been missing something in your life? There is so much more I want to give you if you would only turn and open up to me again. I did not move away from you, but you have put distance between us. This makes everything in your life out of kilter. I will rekindle the passion of our relationship, the fire of my presence in your life. Just ask me and wait in my presence.

**My Prayer:**

# Day Ten

**Scripture:** Luke 3:1–14

**Focus Text:** "And the crowds asked him, 'What then should we do?'" (v. 10).

**Listening to God**: I care about how you live. I created you to reflect my love in the world. No matter what your situation in life, I have marked out this calling for you, a way of life that gives me joy. Are you consciously and intentionally living toward my will for your life? When was the last time you invited me to direct your way? Turn to me now! I can make your crooked paths straight and your rough places like a plain.

**My Prayer:**

# Day Eleven

**Scripture:** Matthew 18:1–4

**Focus Text:** "Unless you change and become like children, you will never enter the kingdom of heaven" (v. 3).

**Listening to God**: When I made you, I wove your spirit together with mine. You will always be my child. The best parent in all the world cannot love as I can love you. My love is unconditional and unbreakable. When you live into this relationship, you fulfill the purpose for which you are placed on earth. Why are you always struggling to be independent? I created you to depend on me and your fellow human beings. It is when you let go and become as dependent as a little child that I can do the most in your life.

**My Prayer:**

# Day Twelve

**Scripture:** Matthew 11:20–30

**Focus Text:** "Come to me, all you that are weary and are carrying heavy burdens, and I will give you rest" (v. 28).

**Listening to God:** Your walk with me was never meant to be a weary slog. If you are feeling worn out and overburdened, check your load to make sure that you are not carrying things I have not called you to carry. When you get in the yoke with me, I always provide what you need to carry the load. When you load yourself up and try to go it alone, I can't help you. Try putting the things that are making you weary in my hands right now. Call on me to do what only I can do. I will give you rest.

**My Prayer:**

# Day Thirteen

**Scripture:** Isaiah 43:1–21

**Focus Text:** "I am about to do a new thing; now it springs forth, do you not perceive it?" (v. 19).

**Listening to God:** Never think you have me figured out. I am always doing something new. If you are too comfortable, you are probably not living close enough to me. Do not resist when life takes you out of your comfort zone. Do not struggle to hold on to the way things are or have been. I am a God of the future, and I am always walking with you into the unfolding surprises of my will. Relax and enjoy the journey!

**My Prayer:**

# Day Fourteen

**Scripture:** 2 Samuel 6:1–7

**Focus Text:** "When they came to the threshing floor of Nacon, Uzzah reached out his hand to the ark of God for the oxen shook it" (v. 6).

**Listening to God**: I have called you to partner with me in my work in the world. But never forget that you are the junior partner. I do not have to have your help. Instead I invite you to join me because I love you. I am the God of the universe. I am in control! When you start thinking you need to fix things, you open yourself up to all kinds of trouble. Today, trust me to be the senior partner in what we are doing.

**My Prayer:**

## Day Fifteen

**Scripture:** Mark 6:30–44

**Focus Text:** "And he said to them, 'How many loaves have you? Go and see'" (v. 38).

**Listening to God**: Miracles happen when you take what you have and put it in my hands. So often you refuse to give me what you have. Usually this is because you feel that it is small, insignificant, even ugly. But I want you exactly as you are. I want the real you. Don't wait until you have achieved some imagined level of perfection to come to me. Do you have fears, doubts, negative feelings, guilt, bad habits? No problem! Bring it on; I can take whatever you give me and transform you to be a blessing to others.

**My Prayer:**

# Day Sixteen

**Scripture:** Hebrews 4:1–11

**Focus Text:** "So then, a sabbath rest still remains for the people of God; for those who enter God's rest also cease from their labors as God did from his" (vv. 9–10).

**Listening to God:** You were created to need down time. Sabbath is my gift to you. Here's a thought: give yourself one day a week when you do only things that feed you and give you joy, and do them with an awareness of my presence. Think it can't be done? Think you are too busy and important to rest? Just give it a try. Taking a Sabbath day every week will fill you with new energy so that the other six days are more productive and joyful.

**My Prayer:**

## Day Seventeen

**Scripture:** James 3:13–18

**Focus Text:** "But the wisdom from above is first pure, then peaceable, gentle, willing to yield, full of mercy and good fruits without a trace of partiality or hypocrisy" (v. 17).

**Listening to God**: Beware of being too sure you are right. Often an unwillingness to yield is linked with a selfish disposition. My wisdom does not push others around or refuse to listen to differing points of view. Human wisdom is often about winning. My wisdom is about healing, saving, and redeeming. Next time someone disagrees with you, be quiet. Put yourself in a listening posture and ask me to show you what is wise and true. This way of being with others bears a rich harvest of good fruit.

**My Prayer:**

## Day Eighteen

**Scripture:** Luke 11:1–13

**Focus Text:** "If you then, who are evil, know how to give good gifts to your children, how much more will the heavenly Father give the Holy Spirit to those who ask" (v. 13).

**Listening to God**: You think you have to understand everything before you can experience it. This misconception robs you of many blessings. There are some things you will never understand until you experience them. And there are some things you are not meant to understand this side of heaven. Instead of always demanding to understand my ways, experiment with trusting me. The best gift I can ever give you is the gift of my Spirit in your life. You don't have to understand it; just ask for the Spirit to come into your life and see what I do. Give me a tiny crack to operate in, and I will transform you.

**My Prayer:**

# Day Nineteen

**Scripture:** Acts 1:1–11

**Focus Text:** "But you will receive power when the Holy Spirit has come upon you; and you will be my witnesses" (v. 8).

**Listening to God:** I pour out my power only on those who are willing to do my will. All too often you work your own agenda instead of mine. This behavior is rooted deep in fallen human nature. If you are not in close communion with me and filled with my Spirit, the work you do for me is of little value in my sight. Relationship must come before work, if the work is to have value. Before you do anything for me, spend some quality time with me. Keep in close touch throughout the day. Then even the smallest thing you do will be a witness to my presence in this world.

**My Prayer:**

# Day Twenty

**Scripture:** John 11:17–44

**Focus Text:** "Jesus said to them, 'Unbind him, and let him go'" (v. 44).

**Listening to God:** You are mine! My deepest delight is to set you free from everything that stunts and binds your life. The tentacles of envy, worry, self-will, and so many other things wrap themselves around your heart without your even realizing it. They steal your joy and make you less effective as my witness. You cannot rescue yourself; they are more powerful than you are. Come to me, and let me free you from the clutches of these spiritual predators. Let me unbind you and set you free!

**My Prayer:**

# Day Twenty-one

**Scripture:** Mark 6:1–13

**Focus Text:** "And he could do no deed of power there, except that he laid his hands on a few sick people and cured them. And he was amazed at their unbelief" (vv. 5–6).

**Listening to God:** Your unbelief can block the good I want to do in this world. I have promised over and over again that whatever you ask in my name I will do. This applies to your life, to those around you, and also to your church and the wider community. If you are dedicated to doing my will, all the power of heaven is at your disposal. Does this mean you will get everything you want? No. That would not be good for you. However, I promise to give you everything you need to live in the flow of my will. Today ask for this and trust me to keep my promise! Your prayers are the channel through which my power flows into the world.

**My Prayer:**

# Day Twenty-two

**Scripture:** 2 Kings 6:8–17

**Focus Text:** "Do not be afraid, for there are more with us than there are with them" (v. 16).

**Listening to God:** You are never alone or outnumbered. Remember how I promised "I will be with you always?" *Always* means right now. It also means tomorrow and every day to come. No matter how powerful your Adversary seems, the armies of heaven are more powerful. I loose those armies to accompany my children on their way in this world. Nothing can defeat you while you hold my hand and rest in me. It's not about how strong you are; it's about how much you trust me. Trust in me with all your heart, and I will bring you through.

**My Prayer:**

## Day Twenty-three

**Scripture:** Luke 14:15–24

**Focus Text:** " 'Come; for everything is ready now.' But they all alike began to make excuses" (vv. 17–18).

**Listening to God:** I have prepared wonderful things for you—a veritable feast of blessings and joys. Why don't you show up to claim them? You keep busy with your "to-do list" and put me last on the agenda. I, however, continue to invite. Try putting the to-do list aside for a while and spend time with me. My greatest gifts are given to those who do this. I can make it all go so much better than you ever dreamed. As you rest in my presence, I will give you everything you need.

**My Prayer:**

# Day Twenty-four

**Scripture:** Matthew 13:31–33

**Focus Text:** "The kingdom of heaven is like a mustard seed that someone took and sowed in his field; it is the smallest of all seeds, but when it is grown it is the greatest of shrubs" (vv. 31–32).

**Listening to God:** You tend to despise small things. This is a mistake. The idea that nothing is worth anything unless it is big is one of the Adversary's lies. This false idea keeps you discouraged and hampers my ability to work through you. When you engage faithfully in the small things I call you to do, I use them for my larger purposes. A word or two spoken at my urging can change a person's life. A small gift of time or attention can rescue someone from hopelessness. You may not always see the results, but trust me to use your small faithfulnesses to bring in my kingdom.

**My Prayer:**

# Day Twenty-five

**Scripture:** Genesis 1:1–25

**Focus Text:** "The earth was a formless void and darkness covered the face of the deep, while a wind from God swept over the face of the waters" (v. 2).

**Listening to God:** In the beginning, my Spirit moved across the dark watery chaos bringing light and order. I can still do this for you today. You may think your situation is totally out of control and beyond help. Or maybe someone else's chaotic life is causing you pain. You may be so immersed in the chaos that you cannot even find words to pray. Don't worry about that. You don't need to tell me what to do. Instead, invite my Spirit to come in and move in the midst of the disorder and pain. I can do more than you could ever ask or imagine.

**My Prayer:**

## Day Twenty-six

**Scripture:** Isaiah 30:15–22

**Focus Text:** "And when you turn to the right or when you turn to the left, your ears shall hear a word behind you, saying, 'This is the way; walk in it'" (v. 21).

**Listening to God:** You may feel that you are alone, but you are not. Do not the let the clamor of the world and the raging of your own spirit drown out the voice of my Spirit within you. You need to listen for me the most when situations are tense and competing voices are loud. As you begin to feel overwhelmed, take time out and let me do my work in you. Here is my promise, and I do not lie: "in returning and rest you shall be saved; in quietness and trust shall be your strength" (v. 15).

**My Prayer:**

## Day Twenty-seven

**Scripture:** Psalm 55

**Focus Text:** "Cast your burden on the LORD, and he will sustain you; he will never permit the righteous to be moved" (v. 22).

**Listening to God**: Why do you try to carry these heavy burdens by yourself? The responsibilities I have placed on your shoulders are meant to be shared with me. The purpose for this sharing is to draw you and me closer together. Out of this deeper relationship you will be able to accomplish far more than you ever could alone. If you do not abide with me and allow me to provide what you need, you will become worn out and embittered. Give this burden to me, and give me yourself too!

**My Prayer:**

# Day Twenty-eight

**Scripture:** Matthew 16:13–28

**Focus Text:** "You are Peter, and on this rock I will build my church, and the gates of Hades will not prevail against it" (v. 18).

**Listening to God:** Never doubt that there is an Adversary who is eager to bring you down and many others with you. In fact, if you are about my business in this world you can expect all kinds of opposition. Don't waste too much time fighting against these things. The opposition is too powerful for you. Instead, trust in my promise that the powers of hell and death will never prevail against my church and my chosen ones. Faithfully put on all the armor that I have provided for you, and the Adversary cannot touch you. Keep on being filled with my Spirit every day, and you will be saved.

**My Prayer:**

## Day Twenty-nine

**Scripture:** Isaiah 64:1–6

**Focus Text:** "From ages past no one has heard, no ear has perceived, no eye has seen any God beside you who works for those who wait for him" (v. 4).

**Listening to God**: I know you hate to wait, but if you are not willing to wait on me, you cannot work with me. If you are not willing to wait, you will rush in and do things that will carry you and your church away from my will. In this dance of life, I am the one who leads. Your job is to follow my guidance as I give it to you moment by moment, day by day. I will lead you, if you are willing to be led. Walk into this day with me. Pay attention to me as I speak, act, and guide. If you do this, you will see me work in ways beyond anything you have ever imagined.

**My Prayer:**

# Day Thirty

**Scripture:** John 10:1–18

**Focus Text:** "I am the good shepherd. I know my own and my own know me" (v. 14).

**Listening to God:** I know you through and through, and I want you to know me. Don't think of me as a holy concept or force. I am a living person right now. Talk to me. Tell me what is on your mind. I don't want to be a stranger to you. Your sin is not a problem with me. I defeated it on the cross, and my Holy Spirit is in the process of rooting it out and destroying it. Spending time with me will help that process along. Give me ten minutes a day, and I will transform you.

**My Prayer:**

## Day Thirty-one

**Scripture:** Matthew 6:5–15

**Focus Text:** "For if you forgive others their trespasses, your heavenly Father will also forgive you; but if you do not forgive others, neither will your heavenly Father forgive your trespasses" (vv. 14–15).

**Listening to God**: When you refuse to forgive someone, you bind that person and the hurt they caused you to your soul. This blocks your spiritual growth and gives the Adversary lots to work with in your life. I cannot bless you as much as I would like if you are holding on to things you should have forgiven. Unforgiveness is poison to your spirit. If you can't bring yourself to forgive, pray to me your desire to want to forgive. I want to set you free. When you let me do that, many will be blessed through you.

**My Prayer:**

# Day Thirty-two

**Scripture:** Romans 5:12–21

**Focus Text:** "If, because of one man's trespass, death reigned through that one man, much more will those who have received the abundance of grace and the free gift of righteousness reign in life through the one man Jesus Christ" (v. 17 RSV).

**Listening to God**: I did not create and redeem you to go through life just barely scraping by. You have received an abundance of grace. It is yours to claim by prayer whenever you want. This grace will enable you to follow my path through any difficulty. This is victory, to follow my path through life no matter where it takes you. If you try to follow a path you make, you will end up bogged down in needless problems and woes. Or you will succeed (by human standards) and become something I never meant you to be. Stay close to me, and you will find abundant life.

**My Prayer:**

# Day Thirty-three

**Scripture:** Ephesians 3:7–21

**Focus Text:** "Now to him who by the power at work within us is able to accomplish abundantly far more that all we can ask or imagine, to him be glory . . ." (vv. 20–21).

**Listening to God:** It grieves me that you think in such cramped terms about what I can do. I am the God of the universe, and I have promised to do whatever you ask in my name. Where is your imagination? Why do you dream so small when the needs around you are so great? And why do you settle for so little of my grace and power in your life and in your church? If you can imagine it, I can do it and more. Spend time with me getting in the flow of my will, then dream big!

**My Prayer:**

# Day Thirty-four

**Scripture:** 1 Corinthians 3:1–15

**Focus Text:** "The work of each builder will become visible, for the Day will disclose it, because it will be revealed with fire, and the fire will test what sort of work each has done" (v. 13).

**Listening to God:** Much is done in my name that has very little to do with me and my purposes in this world. Much energy is spent doing religious activities that will count for nothing in the end. If you are not listening to my direction, your work will not endure, no matter how successful it looks now. You are called to be my disciples. Are you asking my guidance each day about what to do and how to do it? Is what you are doing for your glory or for mine? If you work for yourself, you have your reward. But if you truly work for me by walking with me, your reward will be great in heaven.

**My Prayer:**

# Day Thirty-five

**Scripture:** Micah 6:6–8

**Focus Text:** "What does the LORD require of you but to do justice, and to love kindness, and to walk humbly with your God" (v. 8).

**Listening to God**: I demand integrity from my disciples. You cannot walk humbly with me and walk in arrogance with your brothers and sisters. You cannot be a saint in prayer and a tyrant in your job or with your family. I have given you many things that I intend you to use for the good of those in need around you. The quality of your human relationships shows the true quality of your relationship with me. If you are truly walking with me, I bring you face to face with the needs of my other children. As you treat them, so you treat me.

**My Prayer:**

# Day Thirty-six

**Scripture:** Romans 5:1–11

**Focus Text:** "We also boast in our sufferings, knowing that suffering produces endurance, and endurance produces character, and character produces hope, and hope does not disappoint us" (vv. 3–5).

**Listening to God**: You don't have to go looking for suffering. Life will bring it your way. And if you are faithful to my call, you may have even more suffering than those who are not faithful. Don't be afraid of it. I can do things for you in your suffering that I cannot do otherwise. Suffering strips you of your defenses, your pride, your ability to control things. I can do my best work in you when these things are taken away. I don't send suffering to you or enjoy watching you go through it. But I am able to use it for your good and your growth in grace. Trust me when suffering comes. I will never leave you or forsake you. I will give you gifts as you come through the fire.

**My Prayer:**

# Day Thirty-seven

**Scripture:** Acts 3:1–10

**Focus Text:** "I have no silver or gold, but what I have I give you; in the name of Jesus Christ of Nazareth, stand up and walk" (v. 6).

**Listening to God:** Your lack is never the end of the story. When your resources run out, if you are in the flow of my will, all the resources of heaven are available to you. It grieves me when you forget that I am your source of supply. Praying in the name of Jesus is not magic. It means that you surrender yourself to my will and are willing to be used for my purposes. Let me work through you to do miracles in the lives of others! Together, we can do more than you could ever ask or imagine.

**My Prayer:**

# Day Thirty-eight

**Scripture:** Matthew 6:19–24

**Focus Text:** "No one can serve two masters" (v. 24).

**Listening to God**: You were created to have me at the center of your life. If I am in my proper place in your affection, everything else in your life will be in balance. If you allow any other thing (even good things such as family or church) to move to the center of your life, eventually everything will fall out of balance. You cannot be your own center of gravity. My will is the best thing that could ever happen to you and those around you. I always have your best interest at heart. Can you trust me for this?

**My Prayer:**

# Day Thirty-nine

**Scripture:** 1 Peter 5:1–11

**Focus Text:** "All of you must clothe yourselves with humility in your dealings with one another, for 'God opposes the proud, but gives grace to the humble'" (v. 5).

**Listening to God**: The way you deal with others is a window into your soul. If you are in right relationship with me, you will not need to elevate yourself on the one hand or feel inferior on the other. You will be at ease with others because your worth is rooted and grounded in what I think of you rather than what they think. You will not need to promote yourself if you know in the depths of your heart that I am working out my will for your life. Don't be afraid of people or circumstances that seem to put you at a disadvantage. In my economy, downward mobility is the way up.

**My Prayer:**

# Day Forty

**Scripture:** Malachi 3:8–18

**Focus Text:** "Bring the full tithe into the storehouse, so that there may be food in my house, and thus put me to the test, says the LORD of hosts; see if I will not open the windows of heaven and pour down on you an overflowing blessing (v. 10).

**Listening to God:** If you are going to walk with me, I must own your possessions. If I do not own them, they will own you. I gave them all to you in the first place. Do you understand that? Or is there still a corner of your soul where you hide the idea that you got them for yourself? If you let go of these things, I can use them to bless you. If you hold on to them, they will strangle our relationship. Obey me in giving me one tenth of your income. If you can't do it all right now, start with one per cent a year and work toward the tithe. Put my promise to the test; I dare you!

**My Prayer:**

# Notes

### INTRODUCTION

1. C. S. Lewis, "Footnote to All Prayers," *Poems* (New York: Harcourt Brace Jovanovich, 1992), 326.

### 1. CREATED TO SAIL

1. Parker J. Palmer, *Let Your Life Speak* (San Francisco: Jossey-Bass, 2000), 88.

### 2. THE SAILING LIFE

1. Florida Ellis (unpublished presentation notes on discernment, Atlanta, GA, 2006).

2. Ibid.

### 3. THE WIND

1. Shirley C. Guthrie Jr., *Christian Doctrine* (Louisville, KY: Westminster/John Knox Press, 1994), 292.

2. Ibid., 293.

3. N. T. Wright, *Simply Christian* (New York: HarperCollins, 2006), 136.

### 4. OUR BOAT, THE CHURCH

1. The Nicene Creed, in *The Constitution of the Presbyterian Church (U.S.A.)*, Part I, *Book of Confessions* (Louisville, KY: Office of the General Assembly, Presbyterian Church (U.S.A.), 2004), 3.

### 5. THE CHURCH'S MISSION

1. John Newton, "Amazing Grace," *The Presbyterian Hymnal* (Louisville, KY: Westminster/John Knox Press, 1990), 280.

2. See Robert D. Lupton, *Toxic Charity: How Churches and Charities Hurt Those They Help (and How to Reverse It)* (New York: HarperCollins, 2011).

## 6. THE MAKING OF SAILORS

1. My thinking on the whole armor of God was stimulated by Robert T. Henderson, *The Church and the Relentless Darkness* (Eugene, OR: Wipf & Stock, 2013), 60–85.

2. Ibid., 74.

3. Harry Emerson Fosdick, "God of Grace and God of Glory," *Glory to God* (Louisville, KY: Westminster John Knox Press, 2013), 307.

## 7. FROM ROWBOAT TO SAILBOAT: RAISING THE SAILS

1. Thomas Merton, *New Seeds of Contemplation* (New York: New Directions Books, 1962), 41.

## 8. MOVING WITH THE WIND

1. Thomas G. Long, *Beyond the Worship Wars* (Washington, DC: Alban Institute, 2001).

## 9. PREPARING FOR STORMS

1. Barbara Brown Taylor, *God in Pain: Teaching Sermons on Suffering* (Nashville: Abingdon Press, 1998), 33.

2. The insights in this section are taken from the field of family systems psychology. I find this way of understanding how emotional systems work in churches extremely helpful, especially for leaders. Find a good introduction to family systems for churches in Ronald Richardson, *Creating a Healthier Church* (Minneapolis: Fortress Press, 1996).

# Readings for Further Exploration

$T$he limited scope of this book precludes giving many important topics the attention they deserve. The following lists of books contain resources for going deeper in a number of areas. They do not present a particularly balanced selection of titles. Rather, these are books that have shaped my own thinking in various ways. I cannot put my personal seal of approval on everything in every book listed here. However, they all contain something that has helped me understand what it means to be a sailor in a Sailboat church. I offer them to you along with a saying from the twelve-step movement: "Take what you need and leave the rest." Some of the titles listed here may currently be out of print. However, there are excellent online sources for finding copies of good books that are no longer sold through the usual publishing channels.

If the idea of being a Christian sailor appeals to you, one way to begin the adventure is to select a book listed here and read it thoughtfully in the context of prayer. Ask God to use the book to lead you where God wants you to go. After reading a selection from the book, stop and pray about what the book has stirred up in you, always offering yourself to God to be used for God's purposes. Keeping a journal in which to record your thoughts and prayers enables you to harvest your insights and keep them for further reflection.

Through the miracle of reading, God can use the voices of people who are far away or even long dead to speak God's truth to us today. After you have read a book and found it to be helpful, think about gathering a group of others to read, discuss, and pray over it together. Reading, reflecting, praying groups are one way that God can create in a church a critical mass of people who want to sail instead of row. For this to happen, however, prayer must to go hand-in-hand with reading and discussion. While reading alone can touch the mind and even the heart, it takes prayer to inflame the human will to do God's will.

## PRAYER

Beckman, Richard J. 1994. *A Beginner's Guide to Prayer*. Augsburg Fortress.

Bondi, Roberta C. 1991. *To Pray and to Love*. Augsburg Fortress.

Bourgeault, Cynthia. 2004. *Centering Prayer and Inner Awakening*. Cowley.

Foster, Richard. 1992. *Prayer: Finding the Heart's True Home*. Harper Collins.

Koenig, John. 2004. *Rediscovering New Testament Prayer*. Harper Collins.

Lamotte, Anne. 2012. *Help Thanks Wow*. Penguin.

Maloney, George A., SJ. 1990. *Why Not Become Totally Fire? The Power of Fiery Prayer*. Paulist.

Merton, Thomas. 1971. *Contemplative Prayer*. Random House.

Michael, Chester P., and Marie C. Norrisey. 1985. *Prayer and Temperment*. Open Door.

Murray, Andrew. 1998. "With Christ in the School of Prayer," "The Prayer Life," "The Ministry of Intercession." In anthology *Andrew Murray on Prayer*. Whitaker House.

Rahner, Karl, and Bruce W. Gillette. 1997. *The Need and Blessing of Prayer*. Liturgical Press.

Wolpert, Daniel. 2003. *Creating a Life with God: The Call of Ancient Prayer Practices*. Upper Room.

Yancey, Philip. 2010. *Prayer: Does It Make Any Difference?* Zondervan.

## GROWING IN GOD

Bass, Dorothy C. 2010. *Practicing Our Faith: A Way of Life for a Searching People*. Jossey-Bass.

Bell, Rob. 2012. *Velvet Elvis: Repainting the Christian Faith*. Zondervan.

Bondi, Roberta C. 1987. *To Love as God Loves: Conversations with the Early Church*. Fortress.

Calvin, John. 1984. *The Christian Life*. Edited by John H. Leith. Harper and Row.

Claiborne, Shane, and Jim Wallis. 2006. *The Irresistible Revolution*. Zondervan.

Cordeiro, Wayne. 2008. *The Divine Mentor*. Bethany House.

Enright, William G. 2001. *Channel Markers: Wisdom from the Ten Commandments and the Sermon on the Mount*. Geneva.

Foster, Richard J. 1981. *Freedom of Simplicity*. HarperCollins.

Hollyday, Joyce, ed. 2009. *Clarence Jordan: Essential Writings* (Modern Spiritual Masters Series). Orbis.

Kelly, Thomas R. 1992. *A Testament of Devotion*. Harper Row.

Lamotte, Anne. 2000. *Traveling Mercies: Some Thoughts on Faith*. Pantheon.

May, Gerald 2007. *Addiction and Grace.* HarperCollins.

McNeil, Brenda Salter, Rick Richardson, and John M. Perkins. 2004. *The Heart of Racial Justice: How Soul Change Leads to Social Change.* Intervarsity.

Merton, Thomas. 2007. *New Seeds of Contemplation.* Introduction by Sue Monk Kidd. New Directions Books.

Miller, Paul E. 2001. *Love Walked among Us.* NavPress

Moltmann, Jürgen. 1988. *Experiences of God.* SCM.

Murray, Andrew. 1985. *Experiencing the Holy Spirit.* Whitaker House.

———. 1997. *The True Vine.* Moody Bible Institute.

Nouwen, Henri J. M. 2006. *Spiritual Direction.* HarperOne.

O'Connor, Elizabeth. 1975. *Inward Journey, Outward Journey.* Harper and Row.

Palmer, Parker. 1999. *Let Your Life Speak.* Jossey-Bass.

Peterson, Eugene H. 1988. *Traveling Light: Modern Meditations on St. Paul's Letter of Freedom.* Helmers and Howard.

Strong, Douglas M. 1997. *They Walked in the Spirit: Personal Faith and Social Action in America.* Westminster John Knox.

Thompson, Marjorie. 2005. *Soul Feast.* Westminster John Knox.

Willard, Dallas. 2002. *Renovation of the Heart: Putting on the Character of Christ.* NavPress.

———. 2006. *The Great Omission.* Harper Collins.

## THINKING ABOUT THE FAITH

Bonhoeffer, Dietrich. 1954. *Life Together.* Harper & Row.

———. 1959. *The Cost of Discipleship.* Touchstone.

Guthrie, Shirley C. Jr. 1994. *Christian Doctrine.* Westminster/John Knox.

Henderson, Robert T. 2013. *The Church and the Relentless Darkness.* Wipf & Stock.

Keller, Timothy. 2009. *The Reason for God.* Dutton.

Moltmann, Jürgen. 1992. *The Spirit of Life.* Augsburg Fortress.

———. 1993. *Church in the Power of the Holy Spirit.* Augsburg Fortress.

Packer, J. J., and A. M. Stubbs. 1967. *The Spirit within You: The Church's Neglected Possession.* Hodder and Stoughton.

Stroup, George. 2011. *Why Jesus Matters.* Westminster/John Knox.

Wink, Walter. 1999. *The Powers That Be: Theology for a New Millennium.* Doubleday.

Wright, N. T. 2008. *Surprised by Hope: Rethinking Heaven, the Resurrection, and the Mission of the Church.* HarperOne.

## LIFE IN THE CHURCH

Bass, Diana Butler. 2007. *Christianity for the Rest of Us: How the Neighborhood Church Is Transforming the Faith.* HarperOne.

Callahan, Kennon L. 1994. *Dynamic Worship: Mission, Grace, Praise, and Power.* HarperCollins.

George, Sherron Kay. 2004. *Called as Partners in Christ's Service: The Practice of God's Mission.* Geneva.

Gray, Joan S. 2009. *Spiritual Leadership for Church Officers.* Geneva.

Kirkpatrick, Thomas G. 1995. *Small Groups in the Church: A Handbook for Creating Community*. Alban Institute.

Lupton, Robert D. 2011. *Toxic Charity: How Churches and Charities Hurt Those They Help (and How to Reverse It)*. Harper Collins.

Reese, Martha Grace. 2011, 2nd ed. *Unbinding the Gospel: Real Life Evangelism*. Chalice.

Richardson, Ronald W. 1996. *Creating a Healthier Church*. Augsburg Fortress.

Richter, Don C. 2008. *Mission Trips That Matter: Embodied Faith for the Sake of the World*. Upper Room.

Schnase, Robert. 2008. *Five Practices of Fruitful Congregations*. Abingdon.

Stroupe, Nibs. 2005. *Where Once We Feared Enemies: Inclusive Membership, Prophetic Vision, and the American Church*. CSS.

## FOR SPIRITUAL LEADERS

Baxter, Richard. 2010. *The Reformed Pastor*. Benediction Books.

Benefiel, Margaret. 2005. *Soul at Work*. Seabury.

Collins, Phil, and Paul R. Stevens. 1993. *The Equipping Pastor*. Alban Institute.

Cymbala, Jim. 2008. *Fresh Wind, Fresh Fire*. Zondervan.

Forbes, James. 1989. *The Holy Spirit and Preaching*. Abingdon.

Foss, Michael W. 2009. *Power Surge: Six Marks of Discipleship for a Changing Church*. Augsburg Fortress.

Holmes, Urban T. 2002. *Spirituality for Ministry*. Morehouse.

Johnson, Ben Campbell. 1988. *Pastoral Spirituality: A Focus for Ministry*. Westminster John Knox.

Kroeger, Otto, and Roy M. Oswald. 2012. *Personality Type and Religious Leadership*. Alban Institute.

Neuhaus, Richard John. 1992. *Freedom for Ministry*. Eerdmans.

Nouwen, Henri J. M. 1992. *In the Name of Jesus: Reflections on Christian Leadership*. Crossroads.

Purves, Andrew. 2007. *The Crucifixion of Ministry*. Intervarsity.

———. 2010. *The Resurrection of Ministry*. Intervarsity.

Rendle, Gilbert R. 1998. *Behavioral Covenants in Congregations: A Handbook for Honoring Differences*. Alban.

Wasserman, Dave. 2006. *Azure Wind: Lessons for Ministry from Under Sail*. iUniverse.

White, John. 1986. *Excellence in Leadership*. Intervarsity.

Williamsen, Thomas P. 1997. *Attending Parishioners' Spiritual Growth*. Alban Institute.

Wolpert, Daniel. 2006. *Leading a Life with God: The Practice of Spiritual Leadership*. Upper Room.

## DISCERNMENT

Isenhower, Valerie K., and Judith A. Todd. 2009. *Listen for God's Leading: A Workbook for Corporate Spiritual Discernment*. Upper Room.

————. 2008. *Living into the Answers: A Workbook for Personal Spiritual Discernment.* Upper Room.

Job, Rueben P. 1996. *A Guide to Spiritual Discernment.* Upper Room.

Lonsdale, David, SJ. 1993. *Listening to the Music of the Spirit,* Ava Maria Press.

Morris, Danny E., and Charles M. Olsen. 2012. *Discerning God's Will Together: A Spiritual Practice for the Church.* Alban Institute.

Willard, Dallas. 2012. *Hearing God: Developing a Conversational Relationship with God.* Intervarsity Press.

CPSIA information can be obtained
at www.ICGtesting.com
Printed in the USA
LVOW10s0249160317
527399LV00034B/1113/P